MARK TWAIN

Recent Titles in Greenwood Biographies

J.K. Rowling: A Biography
Connie Ann Kirk

The Dalai Lama: A Biography
Patricia Cronin Marcello

Margaret Mead: A Biography
Mary Bowman-Kruhm

J.R.R. Tolkien: A Biography
Leslie Ellen Jones

Colin Powell: A Biography
Richard Steins

Pope John Paul II: A Biography
Meg Greene Malvasi

Al Capone: A Biography
Luciano Iorizzo

George S. Patton: A Biography
David A. Smith

Gloria Steinem: A Biography
Patricia Cronin Marcello

Billy Graham: A Biography
Roger Bruns

Emily Dickinson: A Biography
Connie Ann Kirk

Langston Hughes: A Biography
Laurie F. Leach

Fidel Castro: A Biography
Thomas M. Leonard

Oprah Winfrey: A Biography
Helen S. Garson

MARK TWAIN

A Biography

Connie Ann Kirk

GREENWOOD BIOGRAPHIES

GREENWOOD PRESS
WESTPORT, CONNECTICUT · LONDON

Library of Congress Cataloging-in-Publication Data

Kirk, Connie Ann.
Mark Twain : a biography / Connie Ann Kirk.
p. cm—(Greenwood biographies)
Includes bibliographical references.
ISBN 0-313-33025-5
1. Twain, Mark, 1835–1910. 2. Humorists, American—19th century—Biography. 3. Authors, American—19th century—Biography. 4. Journalists—United States—Biography. I. Title. II. Series.
PS1331.K57 2004
818'.409—dc22 2004008853

British Library Cataloguing in Publication Data is available.

Library of Congress Catalog Card Number: 2004008853
ISBN: 0-313-33025-5
ISSN: 1540-4900

First published in 2004

Greenwood Press, 88 Post Road West, Westport, CT 06881
An imprint of Greenwood Publishing Group, Inc.
www.greenwood.com

Printed in the United States of America

The paper used in this book complies with the Permanent Paper Standard issued by the National Information Standards Organization (Z39.48–1984).

10 9 8 7 6 5 4 3 2 1

In memory of my brother,
Thomas James Lewis
1946–1991
Backyard humorist, cowboy, and Civil War re-enactor
who exited the stage way too soon

CONTENTS

Series Foreword ix

Preface xi

Chronology xiii

Chapter 1 Introduction: The Man and the Author 1

Chapter 2 A Heavenly Place for a Boy: 1835–1847 5

Chapter 3 From Printer to Pilot: 1848–1861 21

Chapter 4 Lighting Out for the Territory: 1862–1869 39

Chapter 5 The Gilded Years: 1870–1889 57

Chapter 6 Later Years: 1890–1910 87

Appendixes:

A: Clemens Family Tree 105

B: Samuel Clemens's Reading 109

C: Quotable Twain 117

D: Books by Mark Twain 119

E: Important Places and Holdings in Mark Twain Studies 123

Bibliography 125

Index 135

Photo essay follows page 38

SERIES FOREWORD

In response to high school and public library needs, Greenwood developed this distinguished series of full-length biographies specifically for student use. Prepared by field experts and professionals, these engaging biographies are tailored for high school students who need challenging yet accessible biographies. Ideal for secondary school assignments, the length, format, and subject areas are designed to meet educators' requirements and students' interests.

Greenwood offers an extensive selection of biographies spanning all curriculum related subject areas including social studies, the sciences, literature and the arts, history and politics, as well as popular culture, covering public figures and famous personalities from all time periods and backgrounds, both historic and contemporary, who have made an impact on American and/or world culture. Greenwood biographies were chosen based on comprehensive feedback from librarians and educators. Consideration was given to both curriculum relevance and inherent interest. The result is an intriguing mix of the well known and the unexpected, the saints and the sinners from long-ago history and contemporary pop culture. Readers will find a wide array of subject choices from fascinating crime figures like Al Capone to inspiring pioneers like Margaret Mead, from the greatest minds of our time like Stephen Hawking to the most amazing success stories of our day like J.K. Rowling.

While the emphasis is on fact, not glorification, the books are meant to be fun to read. Each volume provides in-depth information about the subject's life from birth through childhood, the teen years, and adulthood. A thorough account relates family background and education, traces personal and professional influences, and explores struggles, accomplishments, and contributions. A timeline highlights the most significant life events against a historical perspective. Bibliographies supplement the reference value of each volume.

PREFACE

This is the third author biography I have written for Greenwood's Biography Series. The series is intended for use by undergraduates and high-school students, but each book is written to be a brief account of the life for the adult general reader as well. To this writer, each subject has presented his/her own particular challenges. Mark Twain was nearly as famous an author in his time as J.K. Rowling is in the early twenty-first century, and this, plus his own public statements about his life and work, have made finding information about his life a fairly easy task. However, unlike the very private Emily Dickinson, for whom much available biographical information is debatable and sketchy even now, the sheer volume of material on Twain makes poring through it another kind of challenge for the biographer.

My method has been to seek counsel from established Twain scholars, gather the most respected source material together, and visit and study at three important locations in Twain's life—Hannibal, Missouri; Elmira, New York; and Hartford, Connecticut. I was also fortunate to be able to examine pages from the original manuscript of *Adventures of Huckleberry Finn* in the Mark Twain Room at the Buffalo and Erie County Public Library. Significant sources used for facts and impressions of Samuel Clemens's life story come from *The Autobiography of Mark Twain*, by Samuel Clemens and edited by Charles Neider; *Mark Twain, A Biography: The Personal and Literary Life of Samuel Langhorne Clemens* in four volumes by Clemens's authorized biographer, Albert Bigelow Paine; *Mr. Clemens and Mark Twain: A Biography* by Justin Kaplan; *Mark Twain: A Literary Life* by Everett Emerson; *The Singular Mark Twain* by Fred Kaplan; Twain's correspondence archived online through the University of California—Berkeley's Mark Twain Project; and firsthand biographical accounts and memoirs from family members and contemporaries such as Clara Clemens, Susy Clemens, Katy Leary, and William Dean Howells. I also found R. Kent Rasmussen's book, *Mark Twain A–Z: The Essential Reference to His Life and Writings* as useful a resource as its title suggests.

I was aided significantly in my research by receiving a Mark Twain Research Fellowship from the Center for Mark Twain Studies. The fellowship allowed me the privilege of staying and studying at Quarry Farm, Samuel Clemens's 20-year summer residence. I thank Jane McCone, Director of the Center for Mark Twain Studies, for her invitation to apply for the fellowship and for her gracious hospitality and helpful assistance during my residency in the autumn of 2003. Quarry Farm preservationist and caretaker, Rick Rolinski, was a steadfast and cordial presence I could count on at the farm during my stay.

Other people who deserve thanks for making contributions, great or small, to my quest for information for this project include Mark Woodhouse, Archivist at the Mark Twain Archives at Elmira College; Margaret Moore, Archivist at the Mark Twain House in Hartford, Connecticut; Vic Fischer of the Mark Twain Papers and Project at the University of California–Berkeley; and Twain scholars Vic Doyno, Michael Kiskis, Ann Ryan, and Barbara Schmidt. Colleagues outside of Twain studies who offered important support include Margaret H. Freeman, Marcy L. Tanter, and Walter Sanders. Talks and presentations I have heard over several years of living a stone's throw away from Elmira, New York, as well as through my membership and participation in the American Literature Association and its conferences, added to my perceptions of this author and his work. In addition, my work benefited from valuable information shared through the collegial Mark Twain listserv—the Mark Twain Forum, and articles such as those published by the Mark Twain Circle and Quarry Farm Papers.

Finally, I thank once again my family, Ken, Ben, John, and my parents, Leonard A. Lewis and Mary A. Lewis, for their enduring love, good humor, interest, and support. I hope this little book may help them all come to know a bit more about our famous "neighbor" who spent so many summers in our area years ago and found it, as I do, an enriching place in which to work.

CHRONOLOGY: ALONGSIDE HISTORICAL AND LITERARY EVENTS

1770	Samuel Clemens, Sam's paternal grandfather, is born in Virginia.
5 March 1770	**Boston Massacre.**
16 December 1773	**Boston Tea Party.**
19 April 1775	**Battle of Lexington and Concord begins the Revolutionary War.**
31 October 1775	Pamelia Goggin, Sam's paternal grandmother, is born in Virginia.
4 July 1776	**Declaration of Independence is signed.**
15 December 1791	**Bill of Rights ratified (first 10 Amendments to the U.S. Constitution).**
11 August 1798	John Marshall Clemens, Sam's father, is born in Virginia.
4 March 1801	**Thomas Jefferson is sworn in as the third president of the United States.**
30 April 1803	**United States makes the Louisiana Purchase.**
18 June 1803	Jane Lampton (Clemens), Sam's mother, is born in Kentucky.
17 May 1804	**Lewis & Clark Expedition begins.**
4 July 1804	**Nathaniel Hawthorne is born in Salem, Massachusetts.**
1807	**Robert Fulton sails the first steamboat, *Clermont*, from New York to Albany.**
11 January 1809	Jervis Langdon, Sam's future father-in-law, is born in Vernon, New York.

19 August 1810	Olivia Lewis (Langdon), Sam's future mother-in-law, is born in Lenox, New York
7 February 1812	**Charles Dickens is born.**
31 May 1819	**Walt Whitman is born on Long Island, New York.**
10 August 1821	**Missouri becomes the 24th state of the United States.**
6 May 1823	John Clemens and Jane Lampton marry.
17 July 1825	Orion Clemens, Sam's brother, is born.
26 October 1825	**Erie Canal opens.**
13 September 1827	Pamela Ann Clemens, Sam's sister, is born.
1828–1829	Pleasant Hannibal Clemens, Sam's brother, is born in Jamestown, Tennessee, and dies at three months.
31 May 1830	Margaret L. Clemens, Sam's sister, is born.
10 December 1830	**Emily Dickinson is born in Amherst, Massachusetts.**
8 June 1832	Benjamin L. Clemens, Sam's brother, is born in Pall Mall, Tennessee.
23 July 1832	Jervis Langdon and Olivia Lewis (Livy's parents) marry and settle in Millport, New York
1835	**Halley's Comet is visible from earth. *Democracy in America* by Alexander de Tocqueville is published.**
30 November 1835	SAMUEL LANGHORNE CLEMENS is born in Florida, Missouri.
1836	***Nature* by Ralph Waldo Emerson is published. Samuel Colt develops the six-shooter revolver.**
1837	***Oliver Twist* by Charles Dickens is published. The telegraph is invented. Queen Victoria ascends to the throne in England.**
1838	**Daguerreotype photography is first exhibited.**
13 July 1838	Henry Clemens, Sam's brother, is born in Florida, Missouri.
1840	Sam begins school in Hannibal.
1841	John Marshall Clemens, Sam's father, sits on Palmyra jury that sends abolitionists to prison. ***The Dial* magazine debuts.**
12 May 1842	Benjamin Clemens, Sam's brother, dies. Orion Clemens, Sam's brother, moves to St. Louis, Missouri. Clemens family sells slave Jennie.
1843	Begins summer stays at the Quarleses' farm near Florida, Missouri. John Marshall Clemens is elected

justice of the peace. **A *Christmas Carol* by Charles Dickens is published.**

1844 **Samuel F. B. Morse exhibits the telegraph.**

1845 ***Narrative of the Life of Frederick Douglass* by Frederick Douglass is published. *The Raven and Other Poems* by Edgar Allan Poe is published.**

27 November 1945 Olivia Louise (Livy) Langdon, Sam's future wife, is born.

1846 Clemens family moves in with local pharmacist, exchanging meals for rent, because of debts. **Sewing machine is invented. Cylinder printing press is developed by Richard M. Hoe.**

1847 ***Evangeline* by Henry Wadsworth Longfellow is published.**

24 March 1847 John Marshall Clemens, Sam's father, dies. Sam begins working in grocery store, pharmacy, and bookstore to help support the family.

1848 Sam begins printing apprenticeship with Joseph C. Amant. **Seneca Falls Women's Rights Convention is held in Seneca Falls, N.Y.**

24 January 1848 **Gold is discovered at Sutter's Mill, initiating the California gold rush.**

1849 ***David Copperfield* by Charles Dickens is published.** Sam's formal schooling comes to an end. **"Civil Disobedience" by Henry David Thoreau is published.**

13 August 1849 Charles (Charley) Jervis Langdon, Sam's future brother-in-law, is born.

6 December 1849 **Harriet Tubman escapes from slavery on the Underground Railroad.**

1850 ***The Scarlet Letter* by Nathaniel Hawthorne is published.**

1851 ***Moby Dick* by Herman Melville is published.**

1852 Sam runs Orion's newspaper in his absence and publishes anonymous sketches of competing editor. ***Uncle Tom's Cabin* by Harriet Beecher Stowe is published.**

1853 Visits and works in New York City and Philadelphia. Reads a great deal at the library in New York.

1854 Visits Washington D.C. ***Walden* by Henry David Thoreau is published. World's Fair in New York City.**

1855 **First edition of *Leaves of Grass* by Walt Whitman is published.** Works with Orion and Henry as a printer in Keokuk, Iowa.

January 1856 Gives first public speech at printer's banquet in Keokuk, Iowa, honoring Benjamin Franklin.

1857 Trains as a cub pilot on several steamboats on the Mississippi.

February 1857 **Supreme Court rules in Dred Scott case, forbidding Congress from banning slavery in states and deciding that slaves are not citizens.**

1858 **Overland stage service from St. Louis to San Francisco begins.**

21 June 1858 Henry Clemens, Sam's brother, dies in Memphis, Tennessee, after being hurt in an explosion and fire on the steamboat, *Pennsylvania*.

1859 Earns pilot's license and makes several voyages on steamboats. ***Origin of the Species* by Charles Darwin is published. *Our Nig; or, Sketches from the Life of a Free Black* by Harriet Wilson is published.**

16 October 1859 **John Brown Revolt in the cause of abolition.**

1860 Works the river as a steamboat pilot. **Abraham Lincoln is elected president.**

1861 **Abraham Lincoln sworn in as president. Civil War begins with attack on Fort Sumter.** Sam hides out for two weeks with a small band of the Missouri State Guard; he does not join Confederate Army. Goes to Nevada with Orion to prospect for silver. ***Great Expectations* by Charles Dickens is published.**

1862 Lives in Virginia City, Nevada, writing for *Virginia City Territorial Enterprise*.

1863 **William Bullock patents continuous-roll printing press.**

1 January 1863 **Lincoln issues Emancipation Proclamation freeing slaves in Confederate States. Homestead Act enacted.**

3 February 1863 Sam Clemens first signs an article using the pen name, "Mark Twain."

1–3 July 1863 **Civil War Battle of Gettysburg, Pennsylvania.**

19 November 1863 **Lincoln delivers Gettysburg Address and issues the Emancipation Proclamation.**

1864	Works as a reporter for the *San Francisco Morning Call*.
1865	***Alice's Adventures in Wonderland*** **by Lewis Carroll is published. Rudyard Kipling is born.**
9 April 1865	**General Robert E. Lee surrenders to General Ulysses S. Grant at Appomattox Courthouse, Virginia, ending the Civil War.**
14 April 1865	**Abraham Lincoln is assassinated at Ford's Theater by John Wilkes Booth.**
18 November 1865	"Jim Smiley and His Jumping Frog" story is published in New York *Saturday Press* and appears nationally.
6 December 1865	**13th Amendment to the Constitution abolishing slavery is enacted.**
1866	Visits Hawaii and writes about it for the *Sacramento Union*. Makes first lecture tour of Nevada and California.
2 October 1866	Gives first public lecture, on the Sandwich Islands, in San Francisco; posters claim, "The Trouble Begins at 8."
1867	Takes tour to Europe and the Holy Land aboard the *Quaker City* with group of religious pilgrims. First book, *The Celebrated Jumping Frog of Calaveras County, and Other Sketches*, is published.
31 December 1867	Meets Olivia Langdon in New York City and accompanies her to Charles Dickens lecture.
4 February 1869	Sam Clemens and Olivia Langdon become officially engaged.
10 May 1869	**Central Pacific and Union Pacific Railroads are joined, creating the first transcontinental railroad.** *The Innocents Abroad* is published.
1870	***Scribner's Monthly*** **debuts. Robert E. Lee dies. Fifteenth Amendment guaranteeing equal voting rights to males regardless of race is passed.**
2 February 1870	Sam Clemens and Olivia Langdon marry in the Langdon family parlor in Elmira, N.Y. Sam is 34; Livy is 24. Jervis Langdon gives Sam and Livy a house on Buffalo's fashionable Delaware Avenue as a wedding gift.
6 August 1870	Jervis Langdon dies in Elmira, New York.
19 September 1870	Emma Nye, friend of Livy, dies in Buffalo.

7 November 1870	First child, Langdon Clemens, is born prematurely and sickly in Buffalo, New York.
1871	Livy recovers from typhoid fever. Sam, Livy, and Langdon move to Elmira, then Hartford. *Mark Twain's (Burlesque) Autobiography* is published. **Stephen Crane is born. *Their Wedding Journey* by William Dean Howells is published.**
1872	Invents self-pasting scrapbook. *Roughing It* is published.
19 March 1872	Olivia Susan (Susy) Clemens born in Elmira, New York.
2 June 1872	Langdon Clemens dies in Hartford, Connecticut.
1873	Co-writes first novel, *The Gilded Age,* with C.D. Warner. Buys land on Farmington Avenue at Nook Farm. Scrapbook is patented and marketed. **St. *Nicholas* magazine debuts. Willa Cather is born. The Remington Company begins making typewriters.**
1874	Publishes "A True Story" in the *Atlantic Monthly. A Gilded Age* is published. *Number One: Mark Twain's Sketches* is published.
Summer 1874	Susan Crane surprises Sam with octagon study at Quarry Farm.
1875	Finishes draft of *The Adventures of Tom Sawyer.* Hires George Griffin as butler for Hartford house.
1876	*The Adventures of Tom Sawyer* is published, first in England, then the United States. **Alexander Graham Bell patents the telephone. Lt. Col. George Custer dies at Little Big Horn.**
1877	*A True Story and the Recent Carnival of Crime* is published. **First public telephones appear in the United States. Edison patents the phonograph.**
17 December 1877	Clemens makes "gaff" speech at poet John Greenleaf Whittier birthday dinner making fun of fellow writers Emerson, Longfellow, and Holmes. The speech is not taken well by the literary establishment.
1878	*Punch, Brothers, Punch! and Other Sketches* published. ***Daisy Miller* by Henry James is published.**
1879	Meets Charles Darwin. Works on *A Tramp Abroad.*

1880 A *Tramp Abroad* published. Invests in Paige typesetter. **New York streets first lit by electricity.**

26 July 1880 Jane Lampton (Jean) Clemens is born in Elmira, New York.

1881 Hires Charles C. Webster, niece's husband, to manage business affairs. *The Prince and the Pauper* is published. ***Uncle Remus* by Joel Harris is published.**

1882 *The Stolen White Elephant, Etc.* is published. **James Joyce is born.**

1883 *Life on the Mississippi* is published. **First skyscraper is built in Chicago (10 stories).**

1884 Founds Charles Webster and Company, publisher. Publishes *Adventures of Huckleberry Finn* in England. ***Oxford English Dictionary* begins publication.**

1885 Publishes *Huck Finn* in the United States, inaugural publication of Clemens's own publishing company, Charles L. Webster Company. Ulysses S. Grant contracts with Webster & Company to publish his memoirs; his death increases sales. Susy Clemens begins biography of her father. Sam begins paying for African American student T. McGuinn to attend Yale University

1889 *A Connecticut Yankee in King Arthur's Court* is published. Theodore Crane dies in Elmira.

Summer 1889 Rudyard Kipling visits Elmira and Quarry Farm.

1890 ***Poems* by Emily Dickinson is published posthumously**.

27 October 1890 Jane Lampton Clemens, Sam's mother, dies in Keokuk, Iowa.

28 November 1890 Olivia Lewis Langdon (Livy's mother) dies.

1891 Closes Hartford house and moves to Europe to save money. **Herman Melville dies.**

1892 *Merry Tales* is published. *The American Claimant* is published. **Edna St. Vincent Millay is born. Walt Whitman dies.**

1893 Serial publication of *Pudd'nhead Wilson and Those Extraordinary Twins* begins.

1894 *Pudd'nhead Wilson* is published in book form. Webster & Co. declares bankruptcy.

1895	World lecture tour begins. *Personal Recollections of Joan of Arc* begins serial publication. ***Red Badge of Courage* by Stephen Crane is published.**
1896	Begins work on *Following the Equator*. *Tom Sawyer Abroad* and *Tom Sawyer Detective and Other Stories* are published. **First modern Olympics held.**
18 August 1896	Susy Clemens dies of meningitis in Hartford.
1897	Family moves to Switzerland and Vienna. *Following the Equator* and *How to Tell a Story and Other Essays* are published.
11 December 1897	Orion Clemens dies in Keokuk, Iowa.
1898	Clemens creditors are paid in full. *More Tramps Abroad* is published.
8 December 1898	Mary Mason Fairbanks dies in Providence, Rhode Island.
1899	*Literary Essays* published. **Ernest Hemingway is born.**
1900	*The Man That Corrupted Hadleyburg and Other Stories and Essays* is published. Whistler paints Sam's portrait. C. D. Warner dies; Sam attends his funeral.
1901	**President McKinley is assassinated.**
October 1901	Receives honorary doctorate from Yale University.
1902	Isabel Lyon becomes Sam's secretary. Livy is very ill. *A Double-Barrelled Detective Story* is published. **John Steinbeck is born. Elizabeth Cady Stanton dies.**
1903	*My Debut as a Literary Person* and *A Dog's Tale* are published. Family moves to Italy. ***The Souls of Black Folks* by W. E. B. Du Bois is published. The Wright Brothers succeed at first powered flight.**
1904	*A Dog's Tale* published. *Extracts from Adam's Diary* is published. Sam begins autobiographical dictation.
5 June 1904	Livy dies in Florence, Italy.
1905	Sam celebrates his 70th birthday at Delmonico's Restaurant, New York City, with literary friends. *King Leopold's Soliloquy* is published.
1906	*What Is Man?* is published. *Eve's Diary* is published. Clemens makes Albert Bigelow Paine his official biographer. *The $30,000 Bequest and Other Stories* is published. ***The Jungle* by Upton Sinclair is published.**

1907	Receives honorary doctorate from Oxford University. *Christian Science* published. *A Horse's Tale* is published. Jean is committed to sanitarium because of her seizures.
1908	Founds "Aquarium Club" with Angelfish. Moves into house in Redding, Connecticut, later named Stormfield. Forms Mark Twain Company. **Richard Wright is born.**
6 October 1908	Clara Clemens marries Ossip Gabrilowitsch.
1909	*Is Shakespeare Dead?* is published. *Extract from Captain Stormfield's Visit to Heaven* is published. Jean moves to Stormfield to help manage household and care for her father.
24 December 1909	Jean Clemens dies at Stormfield.
1910	**W.E.B. Du Bois founds the NAACP (National Association for the Advancement of Colored People).**
21 April 1910	SAMUEL LANGHORNE CLEMENS DIES in Redding, Connecticut. Buried next to Livy, in Woodlawn Cemetery in Elmira, New York.
18 August 1910	Nina Gabrilowitsch, Sam's only grandchild and Clara's daughter, is born at Stormfield, in Redding, Connecticut, four months after her grandfather's death in the same house and on the 14th anniversary of Susy Clemens's death.
14 September 1936	Ossip Gabrilowitsch dies in Detroit, Michigan. As he requested, he is buried at the feet of Mark Twain in Woodlawn Cemetery, Elmira.
11 May 1944	Clara marries Jacques Samossoud.
19 November 1962	Clara Clemens dies in San Diego, California.
16 January 1966	Nina Clemens Gabrilowitsch, granddaughter and last direct descendant of Mark Twain, dies in Los Angeles, California, from a drug overdose.

Chapter 1

INTRODUCTION: THE MAN AND THE AUTHOR

> "Ah, well, I am a great & sublime fool. But then I am God's fool, & all His works must be contemplated with respect."
>
> —*Samuel Clemens*

Mark Twain was a showman and a shaman, a celebrity and a personality, but Samuel Langhorne Clemens, the man behind the showman, loved language even more than he loved people and celebrated the loud intersections of the two, those meetings and crossovers of one over the other, most of all. Clemens wrote novels and lectures, short stories and social commentary, newspaper articles and memoirs, letters and speeches. In each and every one of these forms, he reached out from a now classic American sensibility that was just beginning to form its identity in a larger world. This American character would include a familiarity with the new frontier of the North American continent, a playfulness derived from its youthful rebellion against European rule, guilt over unresolved issues such as race, a fierce individuality especially in relation to government, inherited self-doubt over pedigree and class, and an insatiable ambition to be the biggest, the brightest, and the best while at the same time managing to be the fastest and the richest. Clemens the man was as full of these characteristics as Twain the showman, but Clemens lived the life and wrote the words, then cleverly manufactured the blustery, tough-skinned Mark Twain to do the dirty work of saying the words and ideas out loud on his behalf. If Mark Twain was a caricature whose image appeared on playbills and posters, and went for sale on ticket stubs and in newspaper ads, Samuel Clemens was the artist who introduced an authentic and independent American voice to the rest of the world, probably for the first time.

Clemens described himself for an 1878 passport this way:

> Born 1835, 5 feet, 8–1/2" high; weight about 145 pounds, sometimes a bit under, sometimes a bit over; dark brown hair and red moustache, full face, with high eyebrows and light gray beautiful beaming eyes and a damned good moral character.[1]

Both his overall stature and his hands and feet were described by others as surprisingly small and delicate, showing that his daily work involved the refined tools of pen and ink rather than the rugged equipment of the western trades with which he became so closely associated. His voice was low and slow, full of his mother's Kentucky drawl that breathed life into Mark Twain's many lectures. Reporters reviewing his lecture performances often complained about his slow delivery, accusing him of speaking at the rate of three words a minute. It's probably not stretching the truth to surmise that Clemens liked the sound of his own voice—he liked the sound of the human voice in general, having grown up in the oral story telling tradition of the American South.

His walk, however, was fairly quick and short-stepped. He wrote right-handed and held a cigar that became so much a part of him that when he wasn't puffing on it, it appeared like a sixth finger protruding up from his hand. He could be quick tempered and was capable of holding grudges longer than the Mississippi, but he was also generally sensitive about the underdogs of the world, the downtrodden and defenseless, even though he may not have recognized all of those who were in that condition in his time—people such as the poor, the orphaned, and African Americans he did see; people such as women struggling for the right to vote and Native Americans who suffered from those who had trampled over them going West, he saw perhaps a bit less clearly.

He was a man of his time and country, but most still recognize in the early twenty-first century that he was more than the popular act that Mark Twain put on for audiences. Sam Clemens achieved a literature worth the endurance it has enjoyed for over 100 years, even though much of it is no less controversial now than it was then. The author who claimed that Shakespeare made wine and he made water and that everyone drinks water, wrote works that continue to be enjoyed by the general public today but are now also studied in universities and academic conferences, and are written about in doctoral dissertations and books and articles of literary criticism. Clemens's work is receiving a level of attention and analysis that his pride in his honorary doctorate degree from Oxford University indicates might have equally pleased and amazed him.

In the autumn of 2003, a search of "Samuel Clemens" as subject in the Modern Language Association (MLA) International Bibliography yielded nearly 3,000 books and articles of criticism and scholarship. An Internet search of the same terms called up over 120,000 Web pages. Interestingly, a search of MLA using "Mark Twain" as subject brought only 9 articles and books, but an Internet search of the same terms yielded nearly 3,000,000 Web pages. These numbers indicate that the scholarly community has begun answering for itself the problem of which name to use in seriously discussing the work of this important nineteenth-century author, while the popular media and general-reading public perpetuates Clemens's use of Mark Twain to represent the man and his works around the world. Editors, too, keep Clemens's *nom de plume* on new issues of his many books. It is worth noting that Clemens never published a book only under his own name (though his real name often did appear underneath his pen name). Further discussion of the doubling between the Clemens and Twain can be found in chapter 4.

Whether the dual identity theory resonates with readers, or whether an integrated personality with many facets is preferred, Clemens was a figure who lived nearly 75 years, about 60 years of which were spent in the public eye and nearly 50 years of that under the pseudonym "Mark Twain." As arguably the first American celebrity, Clemens's books and humor became the United States' most well-known export in the late nineteenth and early twentieth centuries. His world tour of 1895 took him to five continents.

In the early twenty-first century, the complexities of Clemens's life and work have remained problematic for scholars, critics, students, and readers alike. The author who did so much to open discussion of race relations in the United States through *Adventures of Huckleberry Finn* and other works is still accused of racism for his use of the "n-word." The man who paid for the education of at least one African American man at Yale is the same man who "collected" adolescent girls as "pets" in the later years of his life. While sympathizing with the downtrodden, Clemens could also be vain and belligerent. In short, behind the celebrity and accolades, Samuel Clemens was a human being who lived and wrote and thought and acted in a very American way—out loud and mostly on his own terms. His life story is an American story—the story of a man for whom the sound of a single voice speaking naturally and truthfully, for good or for ill, meant all.

NOTE

1. Quoted in the Mark Twain Exhibit at Hamilton Hall, Elmira College, Elmira, New York.

Chapter 2

A HEAVENLY PLACE FOR A BOY: 1835–1847

Ancestry interested Samuel Clemens as it did his mother, though the early history of the family lines on both sides is sketchy. On the Clemens side, the name appears in an ancient book by Suetonius that Sam Clemens had in his possession and read up until his death. On page 492 of this volume, a Flavius Clemens is mentioned and described as lazy. In the margin of his copy, Sam Clemens wrote, "I guess this is where our line starts."[1] Laziness was not a common trait of Clemens's namesakes, however; most of their stories are much more colorful. The name itself appeared throughout the Middle Ages and later included at least two popes, Pope Clemens X and Pope Clemens XI. The latter closed the arches of the Roman Coliseum in 1700 so that looters and other criminals could no longer use the ancient structure as a hideout. The pope allowed the amphitheater to become a warehouse for manure used in making saltpeter for a local gunpowder factory. After an earthquake in 1703 brought down three arches of the second southwest ring of the Coliseum, Pope Clemens XI used the fallen travertine to build a monument at the port of Rome.

In England, a landowner named Gregory Clemens became a member of Parliament during the time of Cromwell. This individual signed the death sentence of Charles I and was later tried as a rebel, had his lands taken away, and his head mounted on a pole over Westminster Hall. Gregory Clemens's family may have been the Clemens line that came to America and settled in Virginia, or possibly New Jersey. In Virginia in 1797, the author's grandfather, also named Samuel Clemens, married Pamelia Goggin. On August 11, 1798, the couple had a boy they named John Marshall

Clemens who would grow up to be the author's father. These Clemenses had four other children after John.

When John Clemens was only seven years old, his father died from an accident at a house-raising, leaving John no foreigner to work from that day forward. He was employed as a clerk at an iron factory in Lynchburg. Though his family was not wealthy and his health was not good, John Clemens managed to obtain an education. When his mother married a sweetheart from her youth named Simon Hancock and moved with the other children to Adair County, Kentucky, John went with them and began studying law in Columbia. Later, he served as executor for his father's estate, and when each of his siblings came of age, he doled out their inheritance. His own "inheritance" included a mahogany sideboard and three African slaves. By 1821, he was ready to make a name for himself in the law profession, though his sober disposition did not seem to match his high ambitions for success in a field that meant working so closely with people.

The author's mother, Jane Lampton, took pride in what she believed to be her family ancestry. Her father's side traced their origins to the Lambtons (a slightly different spelling from the Lamptons) who lived in Durham, England, and claimed an earldom in the family. Her mother was of the Montgomery-Casey clan of Kentucky who fought Native Americans for land in that region in the time of Daniel Boone. Jane's mother, Jane Montgomery, claimed to have worn moccasins and saved her own life by jumping a fence while being pursued by Indians. The Montgomery-Casey family lore included many stories of such narrow escapes. As proof of their suppression of the indigenous peoples in these encounters, two counties in the state of Kentucky were named after them.

Jane Lampton was as lively and fun as John Clemens was sober and serious. Her famous son would later say she had a way of being funny without knowing it. Jane was the best dancer in that whole area of Kentucky and loved to dance as late into the night as her family would allow. Her delicate features, fun-loving spirit, sense of humor, and way with a phrase were among the traits that she would later pass down to her son.

Jane loved a physician in Lexington, but following an argument with him, she became engaged to John Clemens out of spite. They were married on May 6, 1823, when John was 25, and Jane was 20. Though she remained loyal to John and never allowed her true feelings about him to directly affect their family, her impulsive actions driven by her emotions would be another trait that she would pass down to the next generation. Over 60 years later, long after John Clemens had died, Jane went to look up the physician at an Old Settler's Convention. She wanted to ask his forgiveness for her rashness after all those years. When she arrived, however, she found that she was too late. The convention had already ended, and the old doctor was gone. Later, Sam Clemens sympathized with the poignancy that moment must have held for his mother. He always spoke more frequently and highly of her than of his father.

One of the traits Samuel Clemens inherited from his father John was his tendency to make poor business decisions. A year after John and Jane married, the Clemenses moved to Gainsborough, Tennessee. In 1825, their first child, Orion (pronounced o-RION) was born. There were not many law cases in such a small town, and neither were there in the next town they tried, Jamestown. In Jamestown, however, John managed to start building his career. He built the first courthouse there, established the county seat, and was elected as the court's circuit clerk.

It was during his reasonable success in Jamestown, Tennessee, that John Clemens purchased a sizable tract of land—75,000 acres—for a sum of around $500. The land lay over the "Knob" of the Cumberland Mountains, about 20 miles south of town. This was John's investment in his family's future. He believed that this purchase that he made for a reasonable price would go up in value dramatically and would secure the family against any financial hardship they might face in the future. He also believed that the value could be counted on as income once miners and developers saw how fruitful the land could be to them. His statement, long handed down in Clemens family lore about what became the mythical "Tennessee land," was, "Whatever befalls me now, my heirs are secure. I may not live to see these acres turn into silver and gold, but my children will."[2] Though the land never provided the wealth John Clemens hoped it would, later his son would use the land in his book, *The Gilded Age*, turning it to gold in a way that his father could never have imagined.

For a time, John and Jane Clemens enjoyed their success in Jamestown. They attended balls and were said to be the best dancers. John was treated locally as an aristocrat. Soon, however, John could see that the progress he had hoped for Jamestown was slow in coming. Unlike the house he built which was more refined, most of the other houses there were still log cabins. Law cases remained few and far between, and the travel required for his work as a circuit clerk wore on his frail health. He turned from law and bought a store but was not successful at that either. In the meantime, two more children were born—Pamela (pronounced Pam-E-la) in September 1827 and Margaret in May of 1830. Declining finances forced him to sell all his inherited slaves but one.

Finally, the Clemenses gave up on Jamestown and moved to a place called Three Forks of Wolf. From there they moved to Pall Mall, Tennessee, on the bank of Wolf River, where John became postmaster. Although the local people coming in and out of the post office called him the dignified title of "Squire" or "Judge," John Clemens's position was less than dignified. He was now in his third profession, with the responsibilities of a father of three children. A fourth child, Benjamin, was born in Pall Mall in June 1832.

John opened a store as part of the post office and moved his family into a log house he had built himself, but again none of these measures seemed to help his financial situation. His health and his dreams were fading. He complained of what would be called migraine headaches today, "sunpain" then, which forced him to avoid the bright rays of the eastern Tennessee sunlight. Nevertheless, John Clemens still had his pride. His tall, thin physique never slouched, and his gray eyes looked out under thick, bushy brows, seemingly right through whoever was the subject of his attention. He did not shirk from what was rightfully his. Family lore tells of his handing his minister a notice to read at the end of services one Sunday that he had lost a cow and would appreciate anyone finding it to return it to him. When the minister forgot to read the announcement, John Clemens stood up and read it to the congregation himself.

Jane Clemens's sister, Patsey Ann Lampton, had married John A. Quarles and settled in Florida, Missouri. Other Lamptons, including the girls' father, Benjamin, and cousin James, joined them. It would not be exaggerating to say that Jane welcomed Patsey and John's invitation to leave their trying days in eastern Tennessee and relocate to Missouri, where they thought they would do better and Jane could enjoy the company of her family. The Quarleses were faring well there with their store and farm. They offered John Clemens a partnership in the store, and the Clemenses packed up their four children and belongings, their one remaining slave, Jennie, and moved to Missouri in the spring of 1835.

Florida was less than 50 miles from the Mississippi River. That and its connections to Salt River made it a promising town for trade. John and Jane moved into a small house in town. Soon, John Clemens took John Quarles up on his suggestion to begin practicing law again. It was into this new start and in the warm company of his mother's family that Samuel Langhorne Clemens was born two months prematurely on November 30, 1835. Later, the author commented on this momentous occasion in this way:

> The village contained a hundred people and I increased the population by 1 percent. It is more than many of the best men in history could have done for a town. It may not be modest in me to refer to this but it is true. There is no record of a person

> doing as much—not even Shakespeare. But I did it for Florida and it shows that I could have done it for any place—even London, I suppose.[3]

They didn't think he would live. The story goes that Jane was so sure of his short time on earth that she let John name the baby instead of naming him herself, as was her custom. John named Sam after his own father, whom he must have barely remembered after his death when John was seven. Langhorne was the name of a close friend from Virginia. They called the boy in his youngest days, "Little Sam." Sometime during that year Halley's Comet streaked across the sky, starting one of the many legends that would grow up about Mark Twain's life. It would be said that the author came into and out of life with the comet, which is essentially, but not precisely, the case.

Trying to make a go of things in their new environment, John and Jane Clemens found themselves very busy, and their children did not receive as much of their attention as they might have liked. John, still trying to make a go of some kind of career, was as sober as ever. In fact, later the famous humorist claimed that he had never seen or heard his father laugh. With a large family to provide for, John built a bigger house in Florida, this time a two-story with an ell that contained a kitchen and dining room. For her part, Jane Clemens was busy keeping up with the family's basic needs. While her sense of humor never left her, getting and keeping her full attention for play and amusement was a challenge in those early days, whether one was the youngest in the family or not.

"Little Sam" stayed under the close eye of Benjamin, three years older, who was often charged with entertaining or helping care for him. In addition, the Quarleses "owned" slaves, and the slaves were often delegated to care for the children of both families. The slaves were among the first voices of influence over Sam Clemens. Both Jennie and another slave known as Uncle Dan'l liked to tell the children stories. From his earliest days, Sam Clemens grew up hearing stories told in dialect and full of enthusiasm and drama. In his autobiography, he writes of his memories of the warmth of the hearth with the children sitting around it listening to long and well-told tales.

In his autobiography, the author remembers one favorite ghost story called "The Golden Arm" that Uncle Dan'l performed in an engaging and frightening manner and that Clemens later retold in his lectures. The story is about a man who married a woman with a golden arm. When the woman died, the man dug up her grave and cut off her golden arm and took it home. One night, the woman, dressed in ghostly white, appeared before the man and demanded to know, "Wheeere's my golden arm? Wheeeeeeeere's my golden arm?" (These lines were performed with increasingly scary voices by the storyteller.) Finally, the storyteller stooped to grab one of the terrified young listeners, shaking him or her about the shoulders and saying, "YOU'VE got my golden arm!" The storyteller then went on to describe how the woman ripped the man to pieces.

Young Clemens never forgot these spine-tingling tales he heard in his earliest days sitting beside his siblings and cousins around the fire of the Quarleses' slave homes. Not only did it press upon him the entertainment value of stories, but the experience also trained his ear for the aural qualities of both dialogue and narration. Capturing this natural quality of language on the written page later became one of Clemens's greatest legacies to American and world literature.

Clemens learned not only to appreciate the stories and voices of his African American friends at the Quarleses' farm but also to know that these people lived in special circumstances that he did not quite understand but that he knew could be quite dangerous. A person was cautioned not to help escaped slaves or voice approval of others who did so, no questions asked. It was a forbidden subject. Slaves were expected to obey a code of conduct that seemed clear only to adults.

The young Sam Clemens witnessed ill treatment of slaves. Once an escaped slave was caught in Florida and tied down by six men in a cabin while his groans and moans bellowed outside to the sensitive ears of the young people listening. Once when Jennie crossed Jane Clemens in a disagreement, the author's mother got out a whip, but Jennie took it from her. When John Clemens answered Jane's call for help and saw Jennie with the whip, he immediately took Jennie by the hands and tied her up by the wrists with bridle reins. Young Sam Clemens watched as his own father struck his friend and caretaker Jennie across the shoulders with the whip. It was just one of the instances from his youth that made a strong and lasting impression on him about race and also about his father.

While his father was stern and reserved, even with his own children, Sam and his siblings enjoyed the good-natured spirit of their Uncle John Quarles. If they were sent to ask him for eggs, for example, he might reply that they should tell their mother to feed her non-laying hens parched corn and march the hens uphill. The children smiled in delight as one of the gullible younger ones among them reported dutifully this ridiculous advice. Uncle John often threatened overly dire circumstances for those who disobeyed his orders, and though the children waited out the day in worried suspense to see what happened if a misdeed occurred, the threats were rarely if ever carried out.

The farm was a wide-open space, with the farmhouse in the middle of a yard fenced-in with logs sawed off at different heights. Hickory and walnut trees provided shade and dropped nuts that the children relished gathering, cracking, and nibbling. A brook wound its way behind the hill in back of the farm, and the children waded there on hot days searching for minnows and other treasures among its deep wells. John Quarles hung swings from the large trees in the pasture. Mary, the slave girl only six years older than Sam, often pushed him, his cousin Tabitha, and the other children in the swings to greater and greater heights.

Adventures seemed never ending on the farm. After the month of April, the children spent days barefoot running through the fields, picking berries and finding nuts, playing as much with one another on the farm as with the children of the slaves in the slave quarters and everywhere in between. Sam and the others liked to ride the horses, play with the other animals, and generally get into trouble with the workday around the farm as much as possible. Food was fresh and abundant—fried chicken, hot biscuits, fresh corn roasted in the husks, Irish potatoes, sweet potatoes, hot rolls, butter beans, roast pig, tomatoes, cantaloupes, peas—and much more. Once, Sam ate several pieces of unripe watermelon and was so taken with cramps that some on the farm thought he might die.

"Sammy will pull through," Jane Clemens said confidently, "he wasn't born to die that way."[4]

Uncle John and the slaves, Uncle Dan'l, Uncle Ned, Mary, Jennie, and others, were approachable and able to hold the children's daily confidences at times in Sam's early life when his mother and father were not. Uncle Dan'l occasionally suffered from lockjaw, a strange malady that fueled the children's curiosity. His kind-heartedness and attention to the children made him a bit of a father figure to them. A very old slave woman seemed so ancient that the children thought the woman lying in the cabin all day had been to Egypt and talked with Moses. They called her Aunt Hannah and believed the bald spot on her head came from fear she experienced watching a pharaoh drown. Many years later, Sam Clemens said that his days spent with the Quarleses, and especially with the Quarleses' slaves when things were running smoothly, were among his happiest as a youth. "It was a heavenly place for a boy, that farm of my uncle John's," the author said.[5]

If John Clemens and his brother-in-law, John Quarles, seemed different in general disposition, they were also apparently different in business practices, because after two or three years, their partnership in the store dissolved, and John Clemens opened his own store across the street while continuing to practice law. He became a justice of the peace, which earned him the title "Judge," which he kept the rest of his life. At 12 or 13, Orion began helping in his father's store. Henry, the Clemenses' last child, was born in July 1838.

When Congress refused to back a program to make navigation on the Salt River more viable, again John Clemens was left with disappointment about the progress of another community. It wasn't long before the first family tragedy struck, which made the Clemenses restless to move on once again.

One day Jane Clemens commented to a neighbor that, so far, her family had been blessed without losing a loved one. That very day in August 1839, according to family legend, little nine-year-old Margaret came home from school ill. Her siblings sat by her bed and tended to her as best they could. During the night, Little Sam, who had been known previously to get up in the night occasionally with bouts of sleepwalking, walked over to Margaret's bed and picked at her blanket. In the morning, Margaret touched the place where Sam had picked her blanket, and the doctor notified the family that Margaret was going to die. In a week, she was gone. The strange coincidence of Sam's sleepwalking venture and Margaret's death haunted the little boy as the story was told over and over again to family and friends. Some scholars today think this incident began what would become Samuel Clemens's lifelong battle with guilt.

Margaret's death and the Salt River situation drove John Clemens to search for another place to live, to make yet another new start. It was almost as though he thought that moving and setting up a new store in a different community would solve any problems the family might have. His search for a town beside a navigable river led him to Hannibal, Missouri, which sat alongside the great Mississippi. Soon, he had the holdings in the Florida store distributed and sold, and the house packed up. With the persistent belief that the "Tennessee land" served as the family's backup security, John and Jane Clemens, their five children, and slave Jennie moved to Hannibal.

At least all five children were supposed to move to Hannibal. It turned out that Orion was never asked to get into the wagon, and the family left without him. The incident was the first of two important abandonments that Samuel Clemens held against his father, mistakes by his father that he recalled even into old age. Orion later rejoined the family but also never forgot his father's omission.

HANNIBAL

Sam Clemens arrived in Hannibal with his family in 1839 when he was about four years old. With the thriving Mississippi in its front yard, Holliday's Hill to the north, and Lover's Leap to the south, Hannibal and its picturesque setting had an established population of the class to which Sam's family belonged. Several families worked in the professions or had a hand in manufacturing; others worked the land with slaves; still others lived in larger houses fashioned in the Greek revival style. There was a sense of the old South about the place mixed with the promise and adventure of the new western frontier. The lively city of St. Louis was only 100 miles away and other interesting locales lay just a boat ride down the river.

If John and Jane Clemens had arrived with more means, they might have fared better in Hannibal sooner, but as it was, they moved with their five children and Jennie into the Pavey Hotel on Hill Street and opened, as usual, a store, which was located on Main Street. Orion was enlisted to tend the store; 12-year-old Pamela and 7-year-old Benjamin went to school. Perhaps he was suffering from the loss of frequent contact with the Quarles family and the trauma of the death of his sister; perhaps it was the loss of Benjamin's companionship during the day or the attention baby Henry demanded from Jane and the transition to the new environment. Some combination of these factors most likely drove Little Sam to become a mischievous handful for his mother and Jennie in Hannibal. The river fascinated him right away, and since it was constantly visible from Hill Street, Little Sam often headed straight for it when no one was looking.

Jane Clemens began treating Little Sam with various kinds of tonics for the troubles of his delicate health, mischievous ways, and odd bouts of sleepwalking. No matter what the doctor recommended or the mother tried, Little Sam seemed headstrong in his quest to find adventure and excitement in his new world. One example of this involved his fascination with measles, which went around town one season. He wanted to experience the illness so badly that he jumped into bed with one of the Bowen boys who had come down with the disease in order to catch a dose for himself. The trick succeeded. Just as he had seen them do for his sister Margaret, the family gathered at his bedside with tears and expressions of concern. The satisfaction Little Sam must have felt over this degree of attention must have been as short-lived as the illness.

Possibly out of sympathy for her difficult but loveable son and perhaps for her own sanity, Jane Clemens began taking the children back to the Quarleses' farm in the summers. For the first such trip, the older children piled into the wagon on an early Saturday morning in June, and Jane held baby Henry on her lap. Sam still lay asleep in the house, and Jane and the others rode away in the wagon. Instead of taking Sam with him as was planned, Judge Clemens later jumped on his horse and took off, totally forgetting

Sam. When he arrived in Florida, Jane confronted the judge, wondering where Little Sam was. Rather than Judge Clemens, it was Jane's brother, Wharton Lampton, who left immediately on horseback for Hannibal to fetch the poor boy. Luckily the house was locked, or Sam might have trotted down to the river he loved so well. Instead, when Uncle Wharton found him, Little Sam was still in the house, crying out of loneliness and hunger. He had managed to pick a hole in a sack of cornmeal to feed and entertain himself during the day. Uncle Wharton took care of Sam and returned him to the Quarleses' farm. No doubt, Orion and Sam talked about their respective abandonments by their father, and this became a bond between them. As for the summers on the Quarleses' farm, Sam enjoyed them for many years, and the annual trips to the farm began a pattern of summer retreats that had importance for the author all of his life.

SCHOOL DAYS

When Sam was about five years old, he began his formal schooling in Hannibal. Under the direction of teacher Miss Horr in the one-room schoolhouse she ran in her log cabin on Main Street, Sam learned reading from a primer through the third reader level as well as geography, mathematics through long division, and lots of spelling and grammar. He learned perhaps a bit less in the areas of self-control and discipline. Sam's conduct in that one-room schoolhouse often ran perilously close to incurring more punishment. He learned early on that punishment applied by Miss Horr was an unpleasant outcome of his actions.

On the first day of school, his behavior had already run the gamut until Miss Horr instructed him to go outside and find a switch for his own punishment. After dismally considering the alternatives available on Main Street, Sam spotted some wood shavings from the cooper across the street and brought one of the flimsy things in to Miss Horr. This mistake was even more dangerous to his self-preservation than the original offense, because he soon found that the switch gleefully chosen by classmate Jimmy Dunlap, who was sent out to provide a more appropriate one for the task, stung with a more distinctive bite.

Sam went home at noon, telling his mother that he no longer wanted to go to school and become a "great man."[6] Instead, he would rather be a pirate or an Indian and scalp or drown people like Miss Horr. Soon afterward, he admitted to his mother, as well, that he no longer believed in praying the opening prayers that began Miss Horr's school day. Miss Horr told the children that if they ever wanted for anything, they should pray, and it would be given to them. This worked one day for Sam when he prayed for gingerbread, and a girl brought some to school then turned her back, which Sam took as his invitation from divine Providence to take what he wanted. When this trick did not work out the next time, Sam told his mother the story of his unanswered prayers, and the devout Presbyterian took pity on him and held him close, saying, "Why Sammy . . . I'll make you a whole pan of gingerbread, better than that, and school will soon be out, too, and you can go back to Uncle John's farm."[7]

While Sammy was beginning to learn hard lessons as a young boy in Hannibal, his family's financial situation was not improving as steadily as his father had hoped. Judge Clemens was elected justice of the peace, but the fees this brought in were low and not steady enough to provide a good income. Times grew so bad that he sold Jennie downriver to keep things going. In those days when slavery was accepted by so many and not questioned, a slave boy was sold by the Methodist minister at the same time and sent downriver, away from his mother. When the Clemenses hired a different slave boy to help out in Jennie's absence, the boy sang nonstop, annoying Sam. Sam complained to his mother about the boy's constant singing, but she corrected him, saying that when the boy was singing, she believed he was coping with the loss of his mother like the boy who was sold down river might do. When he was silent, she said, he must have been overcome with grief. In the strange contradictions of the condition of slavery and the emotions of slave owners, Mrs. Clemens told Sam he should not wish silence on the slave boy. This tolerance and acceptance of verbal expression as a means of easing the strain of slavery's strong hold would come to be of utmost importance in the author's legacy to future generations.

Jennie's sale gave money to John Clemens for a time, and with some of it he bought some rental property on Main Street, but put the rest on credit. Though he had steady tenants, soon they were not paying their rent, and the author's father fell deeper and deeper into debt. He offered to sell so many of their belongings to pay his creditors, even down to the knives and spoons, that soon there was nothing left to sell. Clemens made an expensive trip to Tennessee to see if he could find work there but came home empty-handed. He had tried to buy groceries on credit while he was there, but when the clerk hesitated, Clemens's pride took over, and he slapped the last $5 gold piece the family owned on the counter and headed for home.

During this down period, Sam's 10-year-old brother, Benjamin, became ill and died on May 12, 1842. Despite the tension caused by this and John's costly and unproductive trip to Tennessee, Jane and John stuck together. Orion Clemens claimed that the one and only time he recalled his parents kissing was in comforting each other over beloved Benjamin's death.

The family was aided by James Clemens, a well-to-do cousin from St. Louis, who helped them secure the house on Hill Street in 1844 that is now called Mark Twain's boyhood home. John Clemens opened his law office on nearby Main Street and earned respect for his dignified manner, if not riches from his profession. Jane Clemens took in boarders. For a time, things began to look as though they were leveling out. Sam Clemens was nine years old. This is the period that begins what most have come to know as the Hannibal boyhood days of Mark Twain as they were later expressed in the novel, *The Adventures of Tom Sawyer.*

Several incidents from that novel come out of Sam's experience of middle childhood in Hannibal. Now that he was a bit older, he was out from under his mother's watchful eye a bit more, making trips down to the river, and beginning to grow in awareness about the goings-on in the town of Hannibal. Several of these experiences and incidents made their way years later into *Tom Sawyer* or contributed to shaping the setting of that novel as well as that of *Adventures of Huckleberry Finn*.

One such example involved Sam seeing a man shot on Main Street. When the man was taken home and laid in bed, a heavy family Bible was laid open upside down on his chest, seemingly crushing the breath and life out of him. Though he claims to have never seen an actual slave auction alongside the river, Sam did see black men and women lying chained together on the dock waiting to be sent downriver. Years later, Sam recalled, "They had the saddest faces I ever saw."[8] He witnessed an attack on an abolitionist by townspeople, an action stopped only by the Methodist minister who reasoned with the mob that they should have mercy on the abolitionist, since he clearly must be crazy. He saw a man chase his disobedient daughter through town with a rope coiled like a whip. The girl ran into Sam's own house at his mother's bidding and his mother stood her ground against the man, barring his path through the door. Jane Clemens was not only a good dancer with high spirits and an understanding way with her troublesome son, but she exhibited such courage to Sam that day that she rose even higher in his estimation. He believed she must have had a perfect conscience to perform a feat with such conviction.

No doubt the wild and dark incidents and dangerous events around town fueled the boy's and his friends' curiosity and cravings for adventure. To get out of Sunday school one Sabbath, Sam jumped through his father's office window to wait out his time, only to find the dead body of a man shot on Main Street lying there. The river's constant lure for him finally resulted in his learning to swim after nearly drowning at least twice—once saved by a slave girl and another time by a slave man of the Pavey Hotel named Neal Champ. Sam tried chewing tobacco but didn't stay with it; he admitted later to beginning smoking at the age of nine. Benjamin's death brought Sam and Henry closer, and Sam couldn't resist chances to play practical jokes on Henry. Cats like Peter in *Tom Sawyer* were, indeed, recipients of painkiller, which was originally planned for Sam to ward off cholera. Young Sam did talk other boys into whitewashing a fence for him, much the same way that Tom Sawyer did. He snuck aboard a steamboat at the age of nine as well, but he was soon caught when his legs were spotted sticking out from his hiding place. The boatmen let him out downriver at the town of Louisiana, where Lampton relatives hoisted him by the collar and took him home.

Though Sam was smaller than other boys his age, his imaginative ideas and leadership skills for getting them all in trouble seemed to attract a good number of faithful and fun-loving friends. His gang-about-town grew to include John Briggs, the Bowen boys, Tom Blankenship, and Will Pitts. John Briggs and Will Bowen contributed bits to Sam's character in the invention of Tom Sawyer, though Briggs also stood in as model for Joe Harper in that novel. Tom Blankenship, the son of the town drunk, served as the chief model for Huck Finn, and his cat cries drawing Sam out the window for night adventures made it famously into that novel as well.

The bluffs, river, islands, and nearby cave made the town's natural environment full of possibilities for troublemaking. Several Sundays, the boys climbed Holliday's Hill and threw stones down at people on their way to church. Part of the devilry involved chipping away at a huge boulder they wanted to see roll like thunder to the town below. Finally, they got their wish, and the boulder dropped, snapping off trees and kicking up dust as it rolled. At the boys' call of warning and the sight of the large stone heading down, several people managed to jump out of the way. Finally, the boulder hit a bump and flew directly over a terrified man in a cart and hit a store, causing only minor damage, before it came to rest on a patch of grass. The boulder stayed where it fell for almost 40 years, until it was exploded apart for use in milling.

Swimming in the Mississippi river to Turtle Island, Glasscock's Island (later named Jackson's Island), or the Illinois side, or in the Bear Creek not only cooled the boys off on hot Hannibal days, but it gave cause for some close calls with drowning as well. The boys did not limit themselves to swimming in the summer; they often tried the strength of the river's ice in winter when more close calls risked losing the lives of any or all of them at one time or another. Landing on the islands, just like in the novels, resulted in full-day imaginings of futures as pirates or other adventurers with wide-open free days of fishing and smoking corncob pipes, and not a little worry from their overworked and overwrought adult caretakers. Lying lazily in the sun on the shores of the islands, smoking, and watching the steamboats churn past with cargo and passengers, each one of the boys in the gang wanted the same thing more than anything else in the world—that was one day to be captain of their own ship—each boy dreamed of becoming a steamboat pilot. One or two of them would succeed.

The cave south of town was of particular intrigue as well, as one might expect. The cave was thought to be haunted, and not without good reason. Criminals, runaway slaves, and mysterious characters of all sorts were known to hide there. Perhaps its strangest feature was that the town surgeon, Dr. McDowell, used the cave as the resting place for his beloved 14-year-old daughter. He entombed her corpse in alcohol in a glass cylinder encased in a copper one. The cylinder hung from a beam in the cave. With mysterious enticements such as this, visiting the forbidden territory of the cave became a favorite though terrifying dare among the town's young people.

Sam's friends were not all troublemakers, which showed the complexity of his character right from an early age. He was also attracted to the morally sound and upright youth of his generation. He appreciated those who did well in school, namely Latin star George Robards and his brother, John; Buck Brown who was almost as good a speller as Sam (spelling was his strongest subject in school); and Dr. Meredith's son, John. Though Jimmy McDaniel did not share in Sam's exploits, he was a good contact for another reason—his father was a confectioner, and Jimmy generously acquiesced many times to Sam's requests for samples of the cake and candy he brought to school. There were girls, as well, who pulled at Sam's heart at different intervals—Bettie Ormsley, Artemisia Briggs, Jennie Brady, and Mary Miller. Then there was Laura Hawkins.

Laura Hawkins lived across from Sam on Hill Street, and the two went to school together at Mr. Cross's classroom on the Square. Sam Clemens was as smitten with Laura Hawkins as Tom Sawyer was with Becky Thatcher. Once during a spelling bee, (he famously wore the school's medal week after week for winning them), he purposely missed the first "r" in the word "February" because Laura was the only one left standing as his competitor. Another time, the two were fooling with some building materials outside Laura's new house when a brick accidentally fell on Laura's finger. Sam tended to her "recovery" with great tenderness and care. He never forgot his love affair with Laura, and many of their actual experiences and spats are replayed in *Tom Sawyer*. Sam Clemens's affection for and solicitude toward adolescent girls only began with Laura Hawkins. There was something meaningful to him about innocent, platonic love at the predawn of adulthood that stayed with him and became a joy in his life he tried to recreate again and again.

JOHN CLEMENS'S DEATH

The backdrop of this boy's vibrant youth of school, trouble, and love, remained the ongoing financial problems of his family. Judge John Clemens was strung out once again on credit, owning nothing except the "Tennessee land," which he held onto as something he could pass down as a legacy to his family after he was gone. After leaning on cousin James Clemens heavily for so long, the family finally had to move from their house to share a house with Dr. Grant across the street.

In early 1847, Judge Clemens tried to solve matters once again. An election for the clerkship of Surrogate Court was being held, and Clemens was favored to win if he ran. The position would provide his family with much-needed income, enough most likely to finally establish them financially with their peers in the professions. Rather than take the election for granted, however, John rode from house to house that winter asking for votes. He was elected. On his way to be sworn in in Palmyra near the end of February, he became very ill and had to go home. Orion was summoned from his job in St. Louis, where he had gone to help with the family income, and the family gathered as John's condition worsened into pneumonia. He talked of the "Tennessee land" and how if he had only stayed in Tennessee maybe the family would have been richer. Other than that, he seemed to have no regrets.

"Cling to the land," he said to them.[9] He advised them to let nothing take the precious promise of the Tennessee land away from them.

He called Pamela, now 19, to his bedside. Kissing her for the first time in many years, he said, "Let me die."[10] On March 24, 1847, John Clemens died. Sam Clemens was not yet 12 years old. From that day on, the heavenly place for a boy gave way to a more complicated place for a boy rushing headlong into manhood.

NOTES

1. Qtd. in Albert Bigelow Paine, *Mark Twain: A Biography: The Personal and Literary Life of Samuel Langhorne Clemens*, 4 vols. (New York: Harper & Brothers, 1912), p. 1.

2. Qtd. in Paine, *A Biography*, p. 6.

3. Charles Neider, ed., *The Autobiography of Mark Twain, Including Chapters Now Published for the First Time* (New York: Harper & Row, 1959), p. 1.

4. Qtd. in Paine, *A Biography*, p. 32.
5. Qtd. in Paine, *A Biography*, p. 33.
6. Qtd. in Paine, *A Biography*, p. 38.
7. Qtd. in Paine, *A Biography*, p. 40.
8. Qtd. in Paine, *A Biography*, p. 48.
9. Qtd. in Paine, *A Biography*, p. 73.
10. Qtd. in Paine, *A Biography*, p. 73.

Chapter 3

FROM PRINTER TO PILOT: 1848–1861

As with many families throughout history, the widow Jane Clemens and her children depended on the incomes the children could provide to support them all after their father died. As the oldest and arguably most responsible, Orion had already been working in St. Louis as a printer, sending home money as often as he could. Pamela's knowledge of music enabled her to go to Paris, Missouri, about 50 miles from Hannibal, and teach piano lessons. Jane took in boarders or cooked in exchange for board elsewhere when times became worse. Sam did not want to return to school. He made a promise to his mother at his father's deathbed that he would be industrious and not cause trouble if she would not make him do so.

Though accounts differ as to when the author's formal education actually ended, his mother apparently did agree to his proposal in principle. They made an agreement that Sam would work for the *Hannibal Gazette*, cleaning up around the print shop, while still attending the Dawson school for a time. The newspaper business had helped Orion, so it was perhaps a natural turn for Jane to recommend the same occupation to Sam. Soon afterward he signed on as an apprentice printer with Joseph P. Amant. Amant had recently moved the weekly Missouri *Courier* office to Hannibal from Palmyra. There, Clemens worked with an older apprentice, 18-year-old Wales McCormick, and journeyman Pet McMurry and learned the trade quickly. His excellent spelling skills aided him in setting type. His wages principally consisted of one new suit of clothes and ill-fitting hand-me-downs from Amant or McCormick and food eaten with the Amant family.

Sam proved to be a good worker, now that his work was practical and needed. He ran the printing press while singing songs such as "Annie Laurie," or "Along the Beach at Rockaway." Occasionally, he'd set up and print a poem such as "Blackberry Girl" on silk to give to girlfriends or send to the Quarleses' farm. He didn't go to the Quarleses' farm for summers much anymore, since he'd taken on the responsibilities of a man. Generally, he had one chief task at work a day and could knock off by around three in the afternoon once he had this task accomplished. He still saw Laura Hawkins and went to parties with her and other friends. At times, he needed to find copy as filler for the paper, but the idea of writing filler copy himself seems not to have entered his mind in those early printing days, though that time would soon come.

Walking home after work one day, Sam Clemens found himself kicking a torn page from a book down the street. When he picked it up, he found that it was from a book about Joan of Arc. He started reading and was immediately intrigued by the narration and dialogue of the scene as well as by Joan's courage. As small incidents like this sometimes do, according to Clemens, this experience marked the beginning of his lifelong interest in history and, in particular, fascination with Joan of Arc. From that point forward, Sam found his niche in reading and began devouring history books in earnest. The library John Clemens left to the family consisted of a large Bible, *Webster's Dictionary*, *Nicholson's Encyclopedia*, Woodbridge and Williams's *Geography*, law books, and textbooks he'd probably purchased for the children's use in school. John Clemens had subscribed to the children's periodical, *Parley's Magazine* for his family, and it is very likely that Sam encountered the Massachusetts Sabbath School Society's *Sabbath School Visiter*, edited by Asa Bullard, in the Sunday school classes his mother insisted he attend at the Presbyterian Church. Perhaps history became a subject of interest for young Clemens because it combined stories about people with the kinds of high adventures he craved.

A LITERARY CAREER BEGINS

After Sam had worked for Amant for two years, Orion came back to Hannibal. He believed his family needed him there, and, like his father before him, Orion was still searching for a satisfying career. As a promising intellectual, Orion found printing a step down into the trades from the profession his father enjoyed in the law. He considered law as well for a time, but soon decided to capitalize on the knowledge of journalism he'd learned in St. Louis. He purchased the Hannibal *Journal* for $500 and brought Sam on as a journeyman printer and Henry as an apprentice typesetter. At this time, Henry was 11 years of age.

Henry was not as good at typesetting as Sam had been, even as an apprentice. Sam had to stay late many nights cleaning up Henry's dirty proofs. For some reason, Orion made things difficult for Sam. He rarely praised him for the extra work he performed on Henry's behalf, probably from years of seeing Sam as the black sheep of his siblings. Orion's poor judgment and management skills affected the paper, and subscriptions dwindled. He tried changing the name of the paper and raising the price, but this only made things worse. The sins of the father in terms of losing money in business manifested themselves early on in the sons.

Most accounts place Samuel Clemens's first foray into print at January 1851, when he was 15 years old. Perhaps prophetic of his later works, the short article, titled "A Gallant Fireman," appeared anonymously in the Hannibal *Journal*. Typical of reporters then or since, Sam wrote about a fire that broke out in town, this one in a grocery store next door to the *Journal* office. Interestingly, he used the speech of Jim Wolfe, the printer's apprentice, in colloquial fashion in the article while at the same time making fun of his efforts to put out the fire. These features were another marker of what was to come. He quotes Wolfe, already the victim of many of his jokes outside of print, saying, " 'If that thar fire hadn't bin put out, thar'd a' bin the greatest *confirmation* of the age!' "[1]

The next article attributed to Clemens also appears anonymously, but this time in the *Boston Carpet-Bag*, a weekly humor publication, in May 1852, nearly a year and a half after the first. The gap of time between the articles has not been explained by scholars, though some speculations suggest that Orion may have discouraged Sam from publishing, since he did not publish more of his brother's writing himself. Called "The Dandy Frightening the Squatter," the piece tells of an incident between an outsider arriving in Hannibal wielding a bowie knife and the lesson he learns from a local woodsman. The article is signed, "S.L.C." Another publication from this period appeared a week later, in the *Philadelphia American Courier*. It was called, "Hannibal, Missouri," and again appeared with the author's initials below it. The article contained incidents from the town's history told with humor.

Though he withheld his name, even then, from his published works, Sam Clemens said later that seeing his work "in print was a joy which rather exceeded anything in that line I have ever experienced since."[2] Clemens's reluctance to include his own name in these early publications foreshadows his reliance on pseudonyms later on.

While Sam worked as a journeyman printer for his brother and sent out occasional articles to other publications, business was not picking up for the paper. Things got so bad that Orion made a trip to Tennessee to inquire about the value of the family's mythical "Tennessee land." While he was gone, he left brother Sam in charge of the paper. This simple act may have set in motion the career that would one day catapult Sam to a level of fame and fortune that none of the siblings, much less Sam himself, could have ever possibly imagined.

Sam decided to spice up the paper a bit to increase sales while his brother was away. He self-published four sketches in three issues between September 9 and September 23, 1852. Two of these involved the editor of the competition, the *Hannibal Tri-Weekly Messenger.* It was said that the editor was in love and when his love jilted him, he tried to drown himself in the river. Sam thought the incident was very funny and wrote a sketch describing the editor in detail and telling the story. Another article was written as part of a debate with that paper on the issue of stray dogs barking in Hannibal. Still another article was called "Historical Exhibition—No. 1 Ruse," which anticipates the "Royal Nonesuch" story in *Huck Finn.* Another was "Blab's Tour" about a drunkard's escapade to Glassock (later Jackson's) Island.

By the time Orion returned empty-handed from Tennessee, he found that his paper's circulation had increased considerably while he was away. When he learned how and why, he was faced with the fact that his brother's writing increased sales at the same time that it endangered important business and community relationships. The editor of the *Tri-Weekly*, for example, threatened to tear the *Journal*'s offices apart but ended up moving out of Hannibal entirely to escape the scandal that Sam Clemens's article had helped publicize.

Orion tried a few more things to save the paper. He added a daily edition to his weekly one and attempted to solicit big-name writers from the East to publish in it. Ralph Waldo Emerson, Robert Lowell, and Oliver Wendell Holmes all turned him down. The fact that the New England literati were not interested in a regular publishing contract with a small-town, Western newspaper may have contributed to Sam Clemens's prickly relationship with that group later on when he joined their ranks as an equal.

Orion did allow Sam to keep publishing in the *Journal,* though not without apprehension each time. In November, he published an article called "Connubial Bliss," which was about how bachelors do not have the troubles of marriage to contend with and also about how alcohol can ruin a marriage. Orion gave Sam an "Assistant's Column" to try to channel his efforts and fill pages with copy. In May of 1853, Sam published several sketches in the *Hannibal Daily Journal* and perhaps a poem here or there.

According to Sam's memory looking back at this time in his old age, one poem may have been titled, "To Mary in Hannibal," except that as printer, he put dashes between the "H" and the "l" in the town's name so that the line would fit in a column when typeset. The shortened title became more intriguing, since Mary was apparently not living in a heavenly state.

Business was still bad. After the fire, which had affected the *Journal's* office, the insurance company paid Orion $150 which he used to replace only the equipment that was absolutely necessary. Eventually, when he could no longer afford to pay for their facility, they moved the printing press to the front room of their home, and Orion added an upstairs room. Sam became more and more discouraged. He rarely saw the $3.50-per-week salary Orion had promised him. When Sam asked him for a few dollars to buy a gun, Orion ranted about the expense for such a luxury item. To Sam, it didn't seem like his work or his promise was being acknowledged or rewarded, and he had lots of energy to burn. Secretly, he began planning his departure.

While Orion, Sam, and Henry were trying to keep their mother afloat in Hannibal, Pamela, as the only sibling who had left town, was doing well. In September 1851, she had married a Virginia merchant, William Anderson Moffett, and after a honeymoon at Niagara Falls, the Moffetts opened a grocery business in St. Louis. In September 1852, the couple had a son; in July 1853, a daughter was born. By June 1853, at age 17, Sam Clemens had the notion that life in St. Louis might bear more promise than it did in Hannibal, and he decided to leave the town and his brother's paper.

When he informed Jane Clemens of his decision, the woman who had borne the troublemaking of her son in so many ways and who had liked to dance late at night in her own day, made him hold the Bible with her and make a promise, "I want you to repeat after me, Sam, these words," she said. "'I do solemnly swear that I will not throw a card or drink a drop of liquor while I am gone." Sam took this promise seriously and repeated it back to his mother, word for word. "*Remember* that, Sam, and write to us," she said, and kissed him. Promising to do that too, he took off for St. Louis on the night boat.[3]

When Orion sold the press equipment for the *Journal* for $500, Jane Clemens and Henry moved to St. Louis themselves and together they rented a small house. Sam tried odd jobs in the newspaper business, such as in the composing room of the *Evening News* for a while, but by August of 1853, his restlessness kicked in again, and he was ready to strike out on his own to seek fortune and adventure in the big cities back East. With his small earnings, he bought a train ticket to New York.

While he would later claim that it had been easy to leave Hannibal, the town's scenery, people, and way of life would never quite leave Sam Clemens.

NEW YORK, PHILADELPHIA, AND WASHINGTON, D.C.

He had never ridden a train before, so the experience of riding one for so many days and nights filled Sam Clemens with some pride, if also impatience and discomfort. His first destination was the Crystal Palace in New York City. On his way, he saw Chicago, Lake Erie, Buffalo, Rochester, Syracuse, and Albany, and then sailed down the Hudson River. In his first letter home to his mother, he describes the court house in Syracuse where the "infernal abolitionists"[4] had tried to protect a runaway slave named Jerry McHenry from being returned to a man who lived near Hannibal named John McReynolds. Young Clemens still subscribed to the Southern view of abolition that he inherited. He noticed the different attitudes toward blacks as he journeyed North as well, commenting sarcastically that he should perhaps blacken his face, since blacks seem to fare better than white people in the Eastern states. This was not only Clemens's first venture north, but it was also his first adventure away from Missouri. When he got to New York, he had only a couple of dollars in his pocket and a $10 bill sewn inside the lining of his coat.

Clemens's first "world tour" began with the World's Fair in New York City. He wrote to Pamela about the sights—the flags from around the world, the jewelry and tapestries, the machines. He described the view of the city from atop the Latting Observatory, some 280 feet up. Already he was a travel writer, relating in detail what he saw as he saw it in the letters he promised to write back home. Perhaps the most important sites to Clemens, characteristically, were the new kinds of people he saw and met. To his mother he wrote about seeing two "wild men" from Borneo at the World's Fair, men he said were advertised as being "a cross between man and orangutan."[5] The account, which runs an extended paragraph and relates that Clemens watched the two brothers for about an hour, is often referenced by scholars as important early evidence of Clemens's fascination with race and his desire to write about it. He would go on in a letter a couple of weeks later to describe for his mother the legions of poor children he saw in the city ranging from "mulattoes" and "quadroons" to Chinese. At this time, the homeless children wandering the streets seemed more of a nuisance to him than a cause for compassion and action.

Clemens found work for low wages at John A. Gray & Green on Cliff Street and stayed in a boarding house on Duane. When he wasn't observing the people and sites of the city, such as the ships of New York Harbor, he sat in the Printers' Free Library and Reading Room, close to his boardinghouse, devouring some of the 3,000 books in the collection at that time, which those in the printing trade could read on the premises for free. Clemens had never seen or had access to so many books before in his life.

Despite the theater district and temptations to body and soul that Clemens witnessed around him in New York, apparently he kept the promise that he made to his mother to stay away from drinking and gambling. The prim manners and polite, refined ways he had always envisioned the East having were not what he found in New York. His letters home also expressed concern for his family. By October, though he found that he had "taken a liking to the abominable place,"[6] Clemens was ready to move on once again. His plan for his East coast adventure involved moving south as the weather turned colder in the north. Next he made his way to Philadelphia.

Orion Clemens had always felt an affinity with Benjamin Franklin as a printer, and perhaps it was that familiarity with Franklin and the printing business or the smaller city itself, but the younger Clemens enjoyed the first sampling of Philadelphia. In late October, he wrote his first letter from the city to his brothers, Orion and Henry, describing sites such as Franklin's grave, Independence Hall, and the Liberty Bell (then known as "Independence Bell"). When he saw a bench or pew reportedly sat on by George Washington and Benjamin Franklin in Independence Hall, young Clemens wrote to his brothers "I would have whittled off a chip, if I had got half a chance."[7] He restrained his sampling of history to sitting down on the bench, instead. He was impressed with the finer neighborhoods of Fairmont Hill. The local custom of handing women their purses seemed more in line with what he expected of the East. As a courtesy, men held their purses while women boarded coaches. Clemens was surprised to have a woman hand him her handbag full of money and not expect him, as a stranger, to take off with it.

He found work "subbing" every night as a printer at the *Philadelphia Inquirer,* working from 7:00 in the evening to 3:00 in the morning. Saturday nights he was free to attend the theater. In early December, he wrote a travel letter to the Muscatine *Journal*, Orion's latest enterprise in journalism that he purchased in Muscatine, Iowa. He discovered that Orion had published one or two of his earlier letters. The family's replies to Sam's correspondence had been intermittent since he went to New York, because of Orion's move, with Jane and Henry to Iowa. In his *Journal* letter, Clemens describes Philadelphia as "one of the healthiest places in the Union," a place that "is hard to get tired of...for amusements are not scarce."[8] After writing to Pamela that he hoped to move South before winter set in or come home to St. Louis to get away from working nights, which he said was affecting his eyes, he ended up staying in Philadelphia several more weeks writing letters to the *Journal*. Finally, he made enough money for a visit to Washington, D.C., in February 1854.

In Washington, Clemens, now 18, saw Shakespeare's tragedy, *Othello*, at the National Theater, but he was otherwise unimpressed with the nation's capital. At the time, the Capitol building did not yet have its dome, and the dirt roads had few sidewalks or gaslights. The public buildings were wooden structures. The cornerstone for the Washington Monument had been laid just six years before, and so far, building had progressed to 153 feet with 400 more to go. Clemens watched a debate in the Senate chamber where he saw Senators Douglas and Seward. He also visited the Smithsonian Institution and the Patent Office Museum, where he had the opportunity to see Franklin's original printing press. He marveled at how far the printing press of the 1850s, with which he was so familiar, had progressed since Franklin's time. This attention to the machinations of the printing press and its progress, as well as the new devices he saw on display at the Crystal Palace at the World's Fair in New York, resurfaced many years later with Clemens's interest in the Paige typesetter.

Clemens's visit to Washington lasted four days, then he returned to Philadelphia. A slump in the printing trade left him without a job there or in New York when he journeyed back there looking for employment. He faced the difficult choice of returning to St. Louis and the West, a decision that was eased by the thought of seeing his mother again. Early in April 1854, he rode two to three days and nights sitting upright in a smoking car to St. Louis, where Pamela still lived. After spending a few hours with her, he boarded the *Keokuk Packet* heading upriver for Muscatine, Iowa, saying that his exhaustion drove him to sleep for 36 hours straight. When he reached Orion's house, he found his mother and family at breakfast. He entered the house with a gun in his hand, butt pointing outward. When his mother jumped up in alarm, he told them that he never got money from them to buy a gun so he bought one himself and was about to use it in self-defense.

His mother, who did not like guns, but who was nevertheless thrilled to see her young son who had been away to cities she had never seen, said, "You, Sam! You, Sam! Behave yourself!"[9] He enjoyed the joke, before he fell into her arms, just as glad to see her as she was him. He spent the next several weeks recuperating from his travels in the care of his mother and the company of his brothers.

The next few months found young Sam Clemens working in St. Louis at the *Evening News* again and having more thoughts than success in publishing in the *St. Louis Republican*, though whether this was from his own reluctance to submit pieces there or from their rejection is not entirely clear. In 1855, three travel letters appeared in the Muscatine *Journal*. Orion had married Mary "Mollie" Eleanor Stotts, nine years his junior, in December 1854. Mollie convinced Sam's brother to sell his portion of the *Journal* and move to her hometown of Keokuk, Iowa, where she could have the support of her family with their baby due in September. Orion moved with his young family and bought the Benjamin Franklin Book and Job Office there. Jane and Henry chose to move to St. Louis to be near Pamela. Trying to decide just what he wanted to do, Sam first visited James Clemens in St. Louis, the same relative who had helped his father buy the house in Hannibal and who he hoped would help him hook up with steamboat men to pursue his dream of piloting. James claimed that illness prevented him from introducing Sam to a pilot he knew, and he recommended that Sam stick to the printing trade. Disappointed, Sam went to work at the press on the second floor of the Franklin office in Keokuk. His brother Henry, whom he loved, soon joined him, and the two slept in the print shop as they had years before in Hannibal.

Wages and conditions were no better than they had been when he worked for his brother years before, and this time things were worse because he had less time or ability to write and publish his own pieces. Clemens hated his job and often crossed the river to Warsaw to set type for cash. One of the highlights of his time in Keokuk was the first public speech he ever made. This was a talk at a printer's banquet in January 1856, in celebration of Benjamin Franklin's sesquicentennial birthday. Orion published a review in the *Keokuk Gate City* that said the talk was "replete with wit and humor" and was broken up with several bouts of applause.[10] Longing for adventure, but perhaps remaining there partially for Henry's benefit since their older brother had other responsibilities as a new husband and father, Clemens stayed in Keokuk from July 1855 to October 1856.

Clemens had a few friends who yearned for adventure as he did. He flirted for a time with Annie Taylor, a student at Iowa Wesleyan University whom he met through his sister-in-law, yet romance would not hold him. He dreamed of heading out to see the Amazon River, a desire probably fueled by his reading of a Navy Department report, *Exploration of the Valley of the Amazon*. He was intrigued by Lt. Herndon's reports of coca and the money that could be made from it. Jane Clemens began hearing of Sam's desire to go to South America as he and his partners tried to save up enough money to begin the trip. Longing with friends for a life of adventure on a big river seemed like the old times in Hannibal.

On a stint in St. Louis looking for money to borrow for the trip, Sam attended a fair of the St. Louis Agricultural and Mechanical Association and wrote a piece about it in a letter that he signed "Thomas Jefferson Snodgrass." He sent the travel letter to the *Keokuk Post*, which published it. The *Saturday Post* also picked it up. Clemens returned to Keokuk, hoping that the *Post* might want more of his writing and found that the editor there did, indeed, want to give him a standing order for articles at a sum of around $5 or $10 each. Clemens could make his travels and write back to the paper about what he saw. It seemed that the winds may have turned warmer toward Sam Clemens once again.

Just as in Hannibal when the Joan of Arc article blew against his feet at an opportune time (or just as Clemens would later say it did), another piece of paper blew his way just as he received this writing opportunity. A $50 bill blew against the side of a building in downtown Keokuk. Clemens saw it and grabbed it; he had never seen such a high denomination of money before. He said later that he advertised in the paper for someone who may have lost money, all the while hoping that no one would turn up to claim it. After four days with no one coming forward, he decided the money was his to keep. The money was his signal that it was time to leave Keokuk and seek his adventures on the Amazon.

Clemens began his travels by first going to Cincinnati where he worked for four months as a compositor and continued to publish articles at the Keokuk *Post* under the pseudonym Thomas Jefferson Snodgrass. The money for these pieces was small. One letter called, "A Cincinnati Boarding House Sketch" described a group of people arguing about the existence of God and the soul, along with humorous tall tales. The themes of overhearing stories and writing about such subjects would come back into his work at a time when his readership was much greater, so these sketches provided early practice. He wrote the last of them in March 1857.

In February 1857, at 21 years old and with already over seven years' experience as a printer, Sam Clemens used some of the $50 he had found, boarded the steamboat the *Paul Jones*, and headed for New Orleans on what he thought would be his adventurous trek to that Mississippi of South America, the Amazon River. If a river were indeed calling him, however, Clemens soon learned that it was not the Amazon but instead the great river he had enjoyed so much as a boy.

He made it as far south as Louisville, when the *Paul Jones* ran into trouble getting stuck on rocks. Clemens became fascinated with the goings-on around the boat during the extra days it took to work it free. He loved the language of the sailors and he befriended the pilot, Horace Bixby. Bixby allowed Sam to watch while he steered the boat in the pilothouse. Occasionally he let Sam steer it a bit himself in clear straits. The camaraderie of the ship's men, the lure of the river, and the opportunity to turn the pilot's wheel had a moving effect on Clemens, who had dreamed from his boyhood days on the islands near Hannibal of piloting a steamboat. When they reached New Orleans and Sam discovered that the next scheduled boat for the Amazon River was indefinite if it would ever take off at all, it did not take him long to get back in touch with Bixby.

When Bixby stood inside the pilothouse of the *Colonel Crossman*, turning the big wheel to steer the boat out of New Orleans for the run back up toward St. Louis, Sam Clemens managed to talk him into accepting him as a cub pilot. Bixby charged him $500 for instruction, $100 down with the rest to be taken out of future wages. Clemens did not have the $100, but he had a way with conversation and a love of the river that made Bixby forgive that for the time being. He promised he could get it from his sister's husband, William Moffett, once they reached St. Louis. On March 4, 1857, Sam Clemens joined Horace Bixby in the pilothouse as an official student of the river. When Bixby handed over the wheel, Sam began a formal training that would serve as his college education. He would "major" in the twists and turns and depths of the river and in the human beings of every type he encountered along the lifeline of the United States.

MISSISSIPPI STEAMBOAT PILOT

By the time Sam Clemens got his long-desired wish to be trained as a steamboat pilot, steamboat shipping on the Mississippi River was entering its heyday. When the Clemenses had moved to Hannibal in the 1830s, there were about 200 boats that sailed the river and stopped at the town. By the early 1860s, there were more than 1,000 steamboats carrying cargo and passengers up and down the Mississippi, more than all of the United States' oceangoing vessels combined. Steamboats had flat bottoms and flat sides. They were packet boats, almost like rafts, with elaborate wooden features and trimmings on top that were more decorative than functional. Dangerous hot boilers pumped smoke out two tall stacks into the air. Paddle wheels were built either on the back of the boat (these boats were called stern-wheelers), or on the side (side-wheelers). Side-wheelers were much more common since they were easier to steer; Sam Clemens piloted this kind of boat most of his career.

At the time Clemens took the wheel, steamboat pilots were highly admired and well paid. They earned more money than a boat's captain, about $250 a month, and they did not have to pay board. Clemens was to say later that every kind of human being he met afterward reminded him of someone he had met in his work along the river. Businesses of all sorts, shady and otherwise, set up in river towns where the money and liquor flowed easily. Saloons, prostitutes, the slave trade, and gambling operated alongside more honorable enterprises. Shipping docks kept workers busy preparing passengers and all kinds of goods imaginable for boarding or disembarking.

Pilot Horace Bixby taught Sam Clemens valuable lessons as his hard but dedicated "learner" (meaning teacher) of the river. Immediately he began pointing out physical features of the shoreline to the cub pilot. He made it clear that Sam needed to learn these features by heart not only by day but also by night, by fog, by moonlight, and by starlight and then he needed to relearn how each bluff, inlet, and point looked in all of these conditions floating down the river from the opposite direction. At times, Sam thought the training was hopeless; there was too much to learn, but Bixby encouraged him to start a notebook and jot down every detail until he could remember it on his own from experience. "When I say I'll learn a man the river," Bixby said, "I mean it . . . I'll learn him or kill him."[11]

Just as Sam thought he'd mastered one aspect of the river, Bixby showed him how there were many more things to learn. The depth of the water in each and every spot of the river varied greatly and the depth one day in one spot changed on another day in different seasons of the year and in different weather conditions within the same season. The depth of the river was crucial information for a pilot. Getting it wrong could run the boat aground, and that cost the company money in lost shipping time, repairs, and crew's wages. The frequency of this happening is demonstrated in the fact that a typical steamboat lasted only about five years before it was damaged by groundings, other kinds of collisions, boiler explosions, fires, or other calamities. Profits of the business were so high, however, that a typical new steamboat paid for itself within five months. Still, the successful river pilot with few accidents was highly rewarded, and his reputation on the river exceeded even his high salary. Clemens's regard for Bixby and the profession grew as he watched how well Bixby knew the river and how many close calls they managed to escape with Bixby's knowledgeable hand at the wheel.

As the boat entered shallow water, leadsmen out front lowered lead lines tied with knots at certain intervals to measure the bottom. They called out depths to the "word-passers" on the hurricane deck, who called these up to the pilot. The pilot then made a decision about what to do and called his orders by ringing bell ropes or calling orders down a speaker tube to the engine room where the engineers worked to add or decrease the boat's power. A call of "Maaaaark three" meant the depth was three fathoms, or 18 feet. In a tight spot, every foot of water made a difference. Pilots regularly heard calls such as "Quarter-less-three!" or "Quarter twain!" A call of "Maaaaark twain!" meant the water was two fathoms deep, or 12 feet. This depth "marked" the point where a steamboat coming up on shallow water could go no further without risking damage to the bottom of the boat. It also meant that a steamboat carefully working its way out of shallow water had reached a safe and trouble-free depth. Like everything else on the river, the meaning of the call was more complicated than it first might sound. Emotions ran high in either direction; how a pilot responded to hearing the call "Mark twain!" depended on which way he was headed on the river, whether toward or away from dangerous waters. Samuel Clemens would have been keenly aware of that when he chose "Mark Twain" as his pen name a few years later. Though he may have preferred "safe waters" as the general definition of his pen name, the name, like the river, may have borne more complex stories and meanings.

After Sam trained with him awhile, Horace Bixby took an assignment on the Missouri River and wanted Clemens to go with him. Sam wanted to stay on the Mississippi, so he completed his training under the watchful eye of other licensed pilots. In one assignment, Clemens was sent aboard the *Pennsylvania* as a steersman. The boat made the popular 1,000-mile run between St. Louis and New Orleans under Captain Kleinfelter and was piloted by William Brown. Clemens and Brown didn't get along well, but that turned out to be the smallest disadvantage of the time Sam spent on the *Pennsylvania*. The future author worked with the cantankerous Brown for about 18 months when he suffered one of the most significant losses of his life.

HENRY CLEMENS

Overall, Clemens enjoyed his life on the river so much that he encouraged his younger brother, Henry, who was then about 20, to join the *Pennsylvania* in an unpaid but promising position of "mud clerk." With experience, mud clerks, who checked in freight at remote stops along the river, moved up through the ranks to better positions with pay. Having Henry aboard helped Sam handle his dealings with William Brown a bit better. The brothers had become especially close after the death of their brother Benjamin, though they had their spats as most siblings do. It is said that once Sam dropped a watermelon rind on Henry's head from a second-story window after one of their squabbles. Years later, however, Sam would say that Sid Sawyer in *The Adventures of Tom Sawyer* was modeled after Henry, though Henry was the better boy. Sam was proud of his younger brother, and during their days working on the river, the brothers spent much of their spare time together in the evenings.

One night when they were in port in St. Louis, Sam had a dream about his beloved brother. It was the Clemens custom to say good-bye to family members in the upstairs sitting room. Sam dreamed that Henry was leaving, and his mother followed him to the stairway after saying good-bye. Something made her linger there to watch Henry go down the stairs, and when he reached the bottom, Henry turned and saw her and ran back up the stairs to say good-bye again. Sam went on to dream that Henry had died and was laid out in a metal coffin set on chairs in the upstairs sitting room. His body was dressed in Sam's clothes, and there was a bouquet of mostly white roses on his chest with one red rose in the center. When Sam awoke, the dream seemed so real to him that he started for the house immediately. Running up the stairs two at a time in fear, he dreaded not only seeing Henry's corpse, but also his mother in the pain of grief. When he got there, he was relieved to find no casket stood there at all—it had just been a dream.

Sam did not get along particularly well with William Brown, and when Brown began picking on Henry as well, this aggravated Sam all the more. On the next run to New Orleans, Sam got into a fight with Brown who made him stay onshore in New Orleans to cool off. Sam had a job guarding freight in that city about once a month, so he spent the nights at the job while the boat was still in port. Henry joined him on watch in the evenings. The night before the *Pennsylvania* sailed back North, Sam gave his brother some advice. He told him that if the boat ever ran into any trouble, he should make himself useful by going to the only lifeboat that was tied up on the port side of the wheelhouse and help women and children get into it. Once the lifeboat was full, he should jump into the river and swim to shore because the river was only about a mile wide in most places in the summers.

On the run back to St. Louis with Henry aboard, a boiler on the *Pennsylvania* exploded at Ship Island, south of Memphis. Sam sailed upriver later on another boat and heard bits and pieces about the accident at each port. Once, he heard that Henry was killed. Then he heard that Henry was alive. By the time he reached Memphis, Sam had heard that Henry was there but badly hurt. Sam found his brother lying on a mattress among several dozen burned victims. The insides of his lungs were burned when he inhaled steam. Henry was among those who were not expected to live and as a result was getting less attention and care from the short-handed medical staff. Sam did what he could and managed to enlist the help of Dr. Peyton on Henry's case.

Peyton made no promises, but he treated Henry and announced one evening that he thought Henry had turned the corner and would get better. To keep his progress moving positively, Peyton prescribed a small dose of morphine to keep Henry calm while the men around him moaned on their deathbeds. The tiny dose amounted to an eighth of a grain. Young interns just out of medical school cared for the patients during the night, and Clemens relates that one of them made a mistake in giving Henry his medicine. Not knowing how to measure an eighth of a grain, Sam claims the intern scooped up powder on the end of a knife and gave it to Henry. The amount was a fatally large dose, and Henry died on June 21, 1858. Whether the cause of death was actually an error in administering medicine or the result of Henry's serious burns remains unresolved.

When Sam recounts this tragedy in his autobiography, he returns to the dream he had before that fateful voyage. Henry's body was taken first to the "dead room" at the building in Memphis where the patients were treated. Most of the dead were laid in white-pine coffins, but some elderly ladies in Memphis raised $60 to lay Henry in a metal coffin just like the one Sam had seen in his dream. When Sam entered the room, he saw not only the metal coffin but also that his brother lay in it in Sam's clothes. He watched as an old lady of Memphis placed a bouquet of mostly white roses with one red rose in the center on Henry's chest.

Once they reached St. Louis, Henry's body was removed from the boat while Sam was trying to find his brother-in-law onshore. Sam returned to the boat to find his brother's body gone, so he went back to his sister's house. He stopped men from carrying the casket into the house because he didn't want his mother to see Henry's face, which had become distorted from the opium in the morphine. Sure enough, however, he reported later, when he went upstairs to face her about the accident, there were two chairs in position there ready to support his brother's casket.

Sam never quite got over Henry's death. He had been the one to encourage Henry to work on the river, and yet he was not with him when the accident occurred. The dream and Sam's accounting of it so many years later suggest the closeness he felt with Henry and how he believed he'd failed in his responsibility to their mother to protect her youngest child. Many scholars point to Henry's death as the pivotal tragedy in Sam's adult life that set in motion many elements of his later adulthood as well as certain strains and undercurrents that would run through his writing. There is the character Sid Sawyer, modeled after Henry, for example, in *The Adventures of Tom Sawyer*, and he describes Henry's death in chapter 20 of *Life on the Mississippi*. In *Connecticut Yankee*, character Hank Morgan's planned burning at the stake is held off by the appearance of an eclipse on June 21, the anniversary of Henry's death.

Sam stayed in training as a cub pilot after Henry's death, for two years in all. He earned his pilot license on April 9, 1859, then worked as a licensed pilot for another two years, until May 8, 1861. While he rarely if ever acknowledged his piloting prowess or expertise at the profession, Clemens never had a serious accident and had steady work on the river when many less successful pilots did not. His reputation among his peers along the river was a good one.

Working as a steamboat pilot on the Mississippi River made such a lifelong impression on Samuel Clemens that years later he made a return visit to see how things had changed and then wrote a book about it called *Life on the Mississippi*. Published in 1883, the book is part history, part memoir, and part travel book. Among the most vibrant passages are those in the memoir chapters in which he describes the steamboat itself—the clean, pretty white railings and decorative "ginger-bread" pilothouse, the hurricane deck and the texas deck, the rage of the open fire in the boilers, the way the boat floated peacefully down the river on a calm starry night, the foam the paddlewheel kicked up when it pulled into shore, the sounds of the bell and shouts and busy activity of the crew, the sound of steam screaming through the valves when the boat pulled in. It is clear that Clemens loved not only the river as most readers acknowledge, but also the steamboats on which he made his home for four years. He said later that there was no other occupation in the world than a steamboat pilot in which a man could be more free.

In all, Clemens worked on 18 different steamboats on the river. These included: the *Colonel Crossman* (February–March 1857), *Crescent City* (April–June 1857), *Rufus J. Lackland* (July–August 1857), *John J. Roe* (August–September 1857), *William M. Morrison* (October 1857), *Pennsylvania* (November 1857 and February–June 1858), *D.J. January* (December 1857), *New Falls City* (January 1858, and October–December 1858), *Alfred T. Lacy* (July 1858 and May 1859), *John H. Dickey* (August–October 1858), *White Cloud* (October 1858), *Aleck Scott* (December 1858–April 1859), *J.C. Swon* (June–July 1859), *Edward J. Gay* (August–October 1859), *A.B. Chambers* (October 1859–July 1860), *City of Memphis* (March–July 1860), *Arago* (July–August 1860, and the *Alonzo Child* (September 1860–May 1861).

Clemens continued to work the river until June of 1861, mostly the "lower-river" route sailing back and forth the 1,200 to 1,300 miles from

St. Louis to New Orleans. He was in New Orleans when Louisiana seceded from the Union on January 26, 1861, and his boat was shot at on its way back up the river when he made his departure the next day. The onset of the Civil War brought shipping on the river to a halt and forced Sam Clemens to leave the boats and river he loved so well. Were it not for the war, he may have remained at work as a steamboat pilot for many more years and never have turned back to writing to the extent that he did.

Out of necessity, he left the Mississippi behind him and went off to seek his next adventure. First he joined a Confederate militia in Ralls County, Missouri, as a second lieutenant under the command of General Tom Harris. His commitment, or rather his lack of it, to the Confederate cause lasted only about two weeks. He quit, giving the excuse that the militia's many retreats had exhausted him. The militia disbanded shortly afterward. Clemens wanted no part in the Civil War that ravaged the North and South from the East coast to the Mississippi River, though the poignancy of the severe losses it caused was not lost on him. He once said of President Lincoln's Gettysburg Address, "Mr. Lincoln's words are simple, tender, beautiful, elevated; they flow as smoothly as a poem. This is probably the finest prose passage that exists in the English Language."[12] The Civil War would not be Sam Clemens's calling, but the issues over which it was fought would concern him a great deal in later years.

With the war on in the North, South, and East, Clemens had no future on the river as a steamboat pilot, at least for the time being. It seemed the only place left for the young man to go was to try his hand at new adventures in the Western territories. That's exactly where 25-year-old Sam Clemens—already an experienced printer, journalist, and steamboat pilot—headed next. The Civil War put an end to Sam Clemens's youth in Missouri and his young adult life on America's greatest river, but the Hannibal days were a part of him and the big river continued to flow through his imagination the rest of his life.

NOTES

1. Qtd. in Fred Kaplan, *The Singular Mark Twain* (New York: Doubleday, 2003), p. 43.
2. Qtd. in Kaplan, *Singular*, p. 44.
3. Qtd. in Alfred Bigelow Paine, *Mark Twain: A Biography: The Personal and Literary Life of Samuel Langhorne Clemens*, 4 vols. (New York: Harper & Brothers, 1912), p. 93.
4. Samuel Clemens to Jane Clemens, 24 August 1853.
5. Samuel Clemens to Jane Clemens, 24 August 1853.
6. Samuel Clemens to Pamela A. Moffett, 8 October 1853.
7. Samuel Clemens to Orion and Henry Clemens, 26–28 October 1853.
8. Samuel Clemens to Muscatine *Journal*, 4 December 1853.

9. Qtd. in Paine, *A Biography*, p. 102.

10. Qtd. in Everett Emerson, *Mark Twain: A Literary Life* (Philadelphia: University of Pennsylvania Press), p. 8.

11. Mark Twain, *Life on the Mississippi* (Boston: James R. Osgood, 1883), chap. 8.

12. Qtd. in Jervis Langdon, *Samuel Langhorne Clemens: Some Reminiscences and Some Excerpts from Letters and Unpublished Manuscripts* (Elmira, N.Y.: privately printed, 1935), p. 21.

Samuel Langhorne Clemens in 1870, the year he married Olivia Langdon. Courtesy of the Mark Twain Archive, Elmira College.

Olivia Louise Langdon as a young girl, before Samuel Clemens knew her. Clemens said, "She remained both girl and woman to the last of her life." Courtesy of the Mark Twain Archive, Elmira College.

The farmhouse at Quarry Farm, Elmira, New York. The Clemenses spent 20 happy summers here. The wide veranda looks out over the Chemung River valley and surrounding hills. Mary Ann Cord told Clemens "A True Story" on this porch. Courtesy of the Mark Twain Archive, Elmira College.

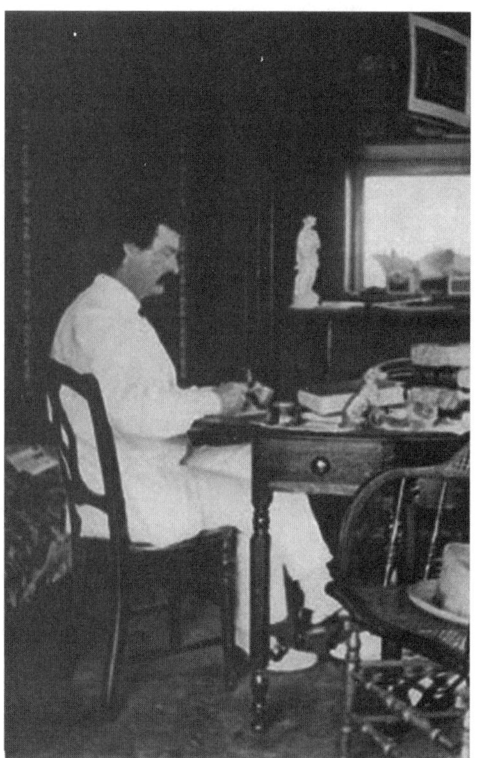

Samuel Clemens writing in his octagonal study at Quarry Farm. Here he wrote most of The Adventures of Tom Sawyer, Adventures of Huckleberry Finn, *and several other books. He wrote, "I haven't piled up manuscript so in years as I have done since we came up here to the farm." Courtesy of the Mark Twain Archive, Elmira College.*

Susy, Jean, Livy, and Clara Clemens, about 1883. Courtesy of the Mark Twain Archive, Elmira College.

Samuel Clemens at his octagonal study, 1903. Courtesy of the Mark Twain Archive, Elmira College.

Samuel Clemens on the porch at Quarry Farm, 1903. Courtesy of the Mark Twain Archive, Elmira College.

Chapter 4

LIGHTING OUT FOR THE TERRITORY: 1862–1869

In *Life on the Mississippi*, Mark Twain summarizes the years after he left the river this way:

> I had to seek another livelihood. So I became a silver miner in Nevada, a newspaper reporter; next a gold miner, in California; next, a reporter in San Francisco; next, a special correspondent in the Sandwich Islands; next, a roving correspondent in Europe and the East; next an instructional torch-bearer on the lecture platform; and, finally, I became a scribbler of books, and an immovable fixture among the other rocks of New England.[1]

The maze of travels and the writing they inspired up to the point of his settling down as a family man and "fixture" of American letters marks the second major period of the author's life. The years out West through his many lecture tours shaped not only much of the content of his writing but also many of his political and social views of the world.

NEVADA AND CALIFORNIA

With the money he'd saved as a pilot, about $800, all in silver coins, and a heavy unabridged dictionary, Sam and his brother Orion, who was still enduring hard and shaky times financially, headed west. Their destination was Nevada, where Orion had secured a post through a friend, Edward Bates, as the Nevada Territory Secretary of the Interior under Abraham Lincoln's administration. They had to pay extra stagecoach fare to bring along the heavy dictionary, but the fact that the reference came along anyway is not only testament to both brothers' love of words (it was Orion's dictionary), but also a kind of promise to themselves that if prospecting didn't work out, they would always have the written word to depend on to make a living. They headed up the Missouri River at a slow pace, according to the recently unemployed steamboat pilot, taking six days to reach St. Joseph, where both the riders of the Pony Express and overland stagecoaches departed for the Western frontier.

It took the Clemens brothers 19 days riding in an overland stage behind a team of 16 horses to reach their destination. They crossed the great plains of the Midwest, through passes of the Rocky Mountains, and across the dusty desert to make the 1,700-mile trip from St. Joseph, Missouri, to Carson City, Nevada. They traveled slowly across rough terrain from sunset to sunset, always heading due west with the sun in their eyes at day's end. One might think that Sam Clemens must have felt dry land was a harsher way to travel than gliding down the easy flow of the Mississippi where he could see the view miles ahead from atop his high perch in the pilothouse. Not so. Instead, Clemens reveled in the new adventure with a characteristic readiness, optimism, and curiosity that would serve him well much of his life. He was young, and had never been this far west of the Mississippi before. If the river had schooled him in the depth of the country at its core, then his travels west were about to teach him the breadth of possibilities that lay across the wide expanse of the continent. In *Roughing It,* an account of his western adventures, Clemens wrote, "Even at this day it thrills me through and through to think of the life, the gladness, and the wild sense of freedom that used to make the blood dance in my face on those find Overland mornings."[2]

At night they put the dictionary in a protected spot out of the way, set their pistols and water canteens close by where they could find them in the dark, and curled up each in his own blanket with a mailbag for a pillow. Sometimes in the night they heard the pounding hooves of the Pony Express thrumming past; the rider made the same trip they were on in just eight days, carrying letters at $5 for postage, each.

On August 14, 1861, the Clemens brothers rode into Carson City and pulled up at the Ormsby Hotel. Orion had his job as secretary to attend to right away and worked to help organize the government of the future state. Eventually he built a large house in town for himself and his family. Sam, however, jumped from job to job. In all, he stayed based in the territory for nearly three years.

After several weeks in Carson City, Clemens went south to Esmeralda in September where he bought claims for himself and Orion. In October and November, he worked as a clerk of the legislature's first session. Come

December, Sam and three companions loaded up mining supplies and walked north to the Humboldt strike district to go silver prospecting. After only two weeks with nothing to show for it, Sam headed back to Carson City, but got waylaid at Honey Lake Smith's inn for nine days when the Carson River flooded and prevented him from returning to the city. He writes an embellished account of his stay there with his various companions in chapters 30 and 31 of *Roughing It*.

By April 1862, Sam went back to the Esmeralda district to develop his and his brother's claims and to mine for silver. For about five months, he lived in a small cabin in the town of Aurora. At this time, there were about 2,000 miners living in the town with more on the way every day. Sam did not have much success as a prospector. He lived most of that time on his brother's money and took a job at a local quartz mill that paid $10 a week. During this time, he began writing humorous letters that he signed "Josh" and sent to the *Virginia City Territorial Enterprise*. The paper liked what he wrote. When his poor finances seemed just about ready to ruin him, the *Enterprise* offered him a job. Sam walked 130 miles from Aurora to Virginia City in September of 1862 to accept his first fulltime job as a newspaper reporter, a position that paid $25 a week and would eventually rise to pay $40.

The *Enterprise* was Nevada's leading newspaper at the time. Joe Goodman, part owner of the paper and the man who hired Clemens, liked Sam's talent but probably also sought favor with Sam's influential brother in government when he hired him, since Orion was in charge of ordering printing jobs for the government. Goodman had just changed the paper from a weekly to a daily paper the year before. The mining boom made the paper more in demand; business in the territory was good.

Sam was treated well at the *Enterprise*. He had the normal assignments of covering local events and sessions of the legislature, but Goodman and others encouraged his talent for offbeat and humorous sketches and stories as well. Within a month of his arrival, for example, the paper published Clemens's "Petrified Man Hoax." The responsibility to cover expected news balanced with the freedom to create his own irreverent art made the *Enterprise* a good training ground for Clemens as a writer, and he stayed with the paper for 17 months.

"MARK TWAIN"

It was during his work for the *Enterprise* that Clemens first used the pseudonym "Mark Twain." On February 3, 1863, a letter appeared in the *Enterprise* that Clemens wrote from Carson City. For some unknown reason, he signed the letter "Mark Twain," and it was printed that way in the paper. Some scholars call this date the birthday of Mark Twain.

While most scholars agree that Clemens took the name from the leadsmen's calls on the river, there are at least two other explanations for the name. One is an explanation that Clemens gave himself years later in an 1874 letter. He claims that he borrowed the pseudonym from a senior pilot named Isaiah Sellers who used to write pieces for newspapers in New Orleans using that name. Clemens had poked fun of Sellers, and according to Clemens, Sellers stopped using the pen name after that. At Sellers' death in 1863, Clemens claims he adopted the pen name since Sellers would not need it any more. The adoption may also have been a tribute to the pilot-writer who had suffered his lampoons.

This explanation may sound plausible except for the lack of research available, even now, to back it up. Sellers did write articles for the New Orleans *Picayune*, but no record has yet been found of his having signed them using the Mark Twain pseudonym. Also, Sellers actually died in 1864, several months after Clemens began using the name in 1863. If Clemens remembered the dates wrong years later, one can only surmise that the story is either another of Twain's many embellished fabrications or that the complete story has yet to be told. There have been some connections drawn by scholars between Clemens and the name from his river days, but so far these findings are inconclusive.

Still another explanation for the name comes from the saloons out West. The story goes that Clemens had the habit of ordering two drinks at once and asked that both (twain) be "marked" on his tab at the same time. It is perhaps not difficult to imagine Clemens, the steamboat pilot turned prospector, sidling up to a bar, raising two fingers, and telling the bartender, "Mark twain."

Whatever the real source of the name that Clemens began using in 1863 may be, over the next several years it became one of the most famous and recognized pen names in all of literature. All of his most well-known works were signed with it (though Samuel L. Clemens often appeared below it in parentheses), and he even adopted it on occasion in correspondence. The name was not used to camouflage his real identity, as *nom de plumes* often do today, but instead it served as a sort of stage name for the author's public persona. Clemens tried to protect its use in later years, when it became obvious that money could be traded using the name. He incorporated the Mark Twain Company in New York in 1908 in this effort. Since then, the Mark Twain Estate has called the name a trademark rather than a pseudonym, providing a fascinating play once again on the word *mark* and the writer's *trade*. The copyright, trademark, and other legal entanglements of the use of the name over the years provided early practice and precedents for the handling of celebrity property in the United States.

Scholars are fascinated by the doubling suggested by Clemens using his real name and Mark Twain almost interchangeably at times, but also by the doubling prevalent in his work (such as the twins in *Pudd'nhead Wilson*) and the divisions of self suggested in his life and writing. An example occurs in chapters 26 and 53 of *Innocents Abroad* when bodies are alluded to being cut "in twain." Some biographers such as Justin Kaplan suggest that Clemens lived a double life of sorts that always required negotiation between the needs and desires of Clemens, the man, and Twain, the public persona. As perhaps America's, and arguably the world's, first celebrity, Mark Twain serves as an early model of the complexities of dealing with that peculiar phenomenon.

The circumstances under which Clemens eventually left the *Enterprise* and Nevada in May of 1864 are unclear. In his autobiography, Clemens claims that Goodman had to leave the area for awhile, and gave Sam the responsibility of managing the paper while he was gone. Not unlike the difficulties in Hannibal when Orion left his paper in Sam's charge, difficulties arose between Sam and the editor of a local competitor. The story goes that the conflict was to be settled by a duel, but that the duel did not happen, and Sam left to avoid getting arrested because dueling was against the law. Whatever the reason, Sam moved further west to California, but he continued to report for the *Enterprise* on special assignment off and on until December of 1865.

In California, Sam wrote for the *San Francisco Call* and was also the *Enterprise*'s Pacific Coast correspondent. While Nevada was silver country, California still attracted gold miners, 16 years after the gold rush of 1848. Sam moved to San Francisco and lived there until late 1866. Based in San Francisco, from December 1864 until February 1865, he went prospecting and writing in Tuolumne and Calaveras counties. From March to August of 1866, he made a trip to Hawaii (then called the Sandwich Islands). If he had no more luck prospecting here than he had in Nevada, it was while Sam lived in California that gold of a different sort finally struck his writing career.

"THE JUMPING FROG STORY"

Calaveras County, California, gets its name from a river that was named after the Spanish word for skulls. In the 1860s, the mining town of Angel's Camp (named "Boomerang" in some printed versions of the story) was the principle village in the county, which was right in the heart of gold mining country east of San Francisco in the foothills of the California Sierra Nevada. While he was prospecting and writing in nearby Tuolumne County, Clemens made a trip to Calaveras County and stayed at Angel's Camp for a month, from late January through late February 1865. As the stories of miners and their lives in *Roughing It* attest, Sam Clemens was listening as he visited these mining towns and prospected. One might say he prospected more for stories than for gold, though if he had found gold, there may have been fewer stories.

One such story Clemens heard was told to him by an old bartender in Angel's Camp named Ben Coon. The story supposedly did happen not far from there and was written up and published in the Sonora newspaper in 1853. After Clemens left Angel's Camp, he began retelling the story, adding embellishments as he went along. He wrote the story down and after several drafts sent a version of it to George W. Carleton in New York for a book that humorist Artemus Ward was putting together. Carlton rejected the story, most likely because the book was too close to press, but he gave the story to Henry Clapp who published it in the *Saturday Press* on November 18, 1865.

The 2,600-word story, then titled "Jim Smiley and His Jumping Frog," was a frame story about a bet. The narrator of the story arrives in a mining town looking for a man named Leonidas Smiley. A bartender tells him that he does not know anyone by that name, but that he does remember a Jim Smiley from some years back, and he can tell the narrator about him if he'd like. The inside story is the tale of Jim Smiley and his jumping frog that the bartender tells the willing narrator.

Smiley was a lucky man, said the bartender. Whatever he placed a bet on—chicken fights, horse races, dog fights—his animal did him proud and won. Now he'd caught a frog and named him Dan'l Webster and had spent several months training him to jump. A stranger arrived in town and could not see anything special about Dan'l Webster. He bet Smiley $40 that any frog could jump as well or better as Smiley's trained one. Smiley took the bet. Since the stranger had no frog, Smiley went out to catch him one. While he was gone, the stranger opened Dan'l Webster's mouth and filled him with quail shot. The bartender then tells the narrator of the frame story how the jumping race took place when Smiley returned and what happened next. Before he can launch very far into another tale about Jim Smiley, however, the narrator escapes and continues on his way.

Contemporary scholars call this classic Mark Twain story simply "the jumping frog story" because it went through so many revisions and alternate titles during its publication history. In Clemens's first book, for example, the story's title changed to "The Celebrated Jumping Frog of Calaveras County." In another book eight years later, the story was written in English, then badly translated into French, then translated back to English—all as a ruse by Clemens playing with language. Its title became "The Jumping Frog in English, Then in French, Then Clawed Back into a Civilized Language Once More by Patient, Unremunerated Toil." In 1894, Clemens revamped the story again to include its "origins" from the ancient Greek, and it appeared in the *North American Review* as "The Private History of the Jumping Frog Story." Coincidentally, and without Clemens's knowledge at the time, a Greek scholar had translated the jumping frog story for use in a Greek textbook. By 1903, Harper publishers collected the previous versions and published them together. They called the collection, *The Jumping Frog in English, Then in French, Then Clawed Back into a Civilized Language Once Again by Patient, Unremunerated Toil.*

The story was an instant hit and gave Mark Twain national attention as a humorous writer. It got picked up by several newspapers and magazines along the East coast, including those in the largest cities. The recognition was a boost to Clemens's writing career. Although he was still an obscure writer from out West, the success of the story encouraged a publisher to help him produce his first book.

In early 1867, Charles H. Webb suggested to Clemens that he put together the jumping frog story with some other sketches and publish them together as a book. Webb helped him edit the manuscript and landed Clemens an appointment with the same George Carleton who had passed on the story the first time when Clapp's book was about to go to press. Carleton rose to meet Clemens in his office and when he understood what Clemens was there to ask, he waved his arm all around the room and said, "Books—look at those shelves! Every one of them is loaded with books that are waiting for publication. Do I want any more? Excuse me, I don't. Good morning."[3]

It turned out that Webb published the book of sketches himself with an attractive cover that Clemens liked, but over 20 years later, the famous Mark Twain had an encounter of a different sort with George Carleton. Clemens records in his autobiography that he was staying with his family at the Schweizerhof, in Lucerne, when Carleton dropped by. Without wasting time on small talk, Carleton immediately got to the point of settling the old score from 20 years ago. He said, "I am substantially an obscure person but I have a couple of such colossal distinctions to my credit that I am entitled to immortality—to wit: I refused a book of yours and for this I stand without competitor as the prize ass of the nineteenth century."[4] Clemens states that he was so impressed by Carleton's apology that he admitted he had killed him several times over in his dreams over the last 20 years but from that moment on he regarded him as a friend and promised not to kill him any more.

Clemens wrote for several newspapers while he lived in San Francisco, including the *San Francisco Call*, the *San Francisco Trade Union*, the *San Francisco Alta California*, and the *San Francisco Dramatic Chronicle*. During his years there, he became friends with several other writers in the city, including Bret Harte, Joaquin Miller, Charles Henry Webb, and Charles Warren Stoddard, among others. After his trips to the mines, Clemens soon found that he needed stimulation to keep coming up with new subjects for his writing. He began to miss his piloting days.

In February 1866, the prestigious *Sacramento Union* hired Clemens to write travel letters if he would take a trip to the Sandwich Islands (Hawaii), a location that had grown increasingly intriguing for California residents. He sailed off for the islands with great excitement and anticipation aboard the *Ajax* on March 7, 1866, and was soon taking notes in a notebook. It took 11 days to reach Honolulu. Clemens intended to stay for one month, but ended up sampling the adventures of the islands and writing them down for four months and one day.

Using his observations and his notebook, Clemens wrote the *Union* 25 letters in all, or about 90,000 words. When he returned from the islands, Clemens found that his humorous travel letters in the *Union* had been highly popular. He hoped to compile his writing into a book about the adventure but could not find an interested publisher. Instead, years later he reworked the material and added it to *Roughing It* as chapters 62–77.

Possibly the most important outcome of Clemens's Hawaiian travels did not relate as much to his writing as it did to yet another career to add to his growing list—printer, steamboat pilot, prospector, journalist, and now lecturer. The man who had spent so much time listening to the voices he'd heard across America and on the islands in the Pacific was about to tell what he'd heard to an eager and welcoming audience.

LECTURE TOURS

Mark Twain gave his first professional lecture on October 2, 1866, at Maguire's Opera House in San Francisco. The topic was "Our Fellow Savages of the Sandwich Islands." Advertisements for the lecture bore headlines for such amazements as "A Den of Ferocious Wild Beasts,"

"Magnificent Fireworks," and "A Grand Torchlight Procession" but the fine print told the audience that, well, each of these was not actually taking place for various reasons, but what was taking place would equally satisfy their hunger for entertainment. The lines at the bottom of the ad piqued audience interest even further by promising "The doors open at 7 o'clock. The trouble begins at 8." The phrase became synonymous with Twain's many lecture tours that occurred on and off for nearly the next 30 years.

At age 30, Clemens did not know what to expect that first night in 1866. He did not think many people would come to hear him. He had given an informal talk before at the Iowa printer's dinner in Keokuk celebrating Benjamin Franklin's birthday and a few others at Carson City's Third House burlesque. However, this was the first time an audience was paying for tickets solely to hear him speak. He envisioned walking out on the stage to face an auditorium of empty seats, but when he arrived at the theater and saw the completely packed house, he was nearly overcome with stage fright. From somewhere inside himself, probably just below the surface, Sam Clemens pulled up the courage to walk onto the stage and deliver a humorous lecture about what he saw in the Sandwich Islands—something akin to a "stand up" comedy routine today. The result could not be called anything short of a resounding success. That night launched a career that would bail Clemens out of financial straits more than once in his life.

In May 1866 Clemens was given the opportunity by a friend, Frank Fuller, who had moved back East, to speak at a much larger forum, the Cooper Union in New York City. Clemens accepted the offer but was terrified of the performance. He knew that if he were a hit in New York, then he had a lucrative career in lecturing for the taking. After his first tour of Nevada and California, he also lectured in the friendly regions of Missouri and the Midwest to practice before going to New York.

Fuller advertised the event well. He appealed to Californians living in the city but also appealed to fellow journalists to play up the event ahead of time. Journalists knew the public. They knew that people of that time needed a better reason than simply entertainment to pay for tickets to come out and hear a lecture, so in one article, a reviewer promised that the lecture would be full of information about the far-away Sandwich Islands. Despite all the advance publicity, Clemens worried that Easterners were a very different kind of audience indeed and had access to every possible venue of information and entertainment, that they would not come out for a relatively unknown speaker from the other side of the country. In fear of speaking to an empty house, he asked Fuller to hand out free tickets to schoolteachers. He needn't have worried. Fuller's strategy worked, and the Cooper Union was not only so packed that they had to turn people away, but Clemens's unique blend of a humorous yet informative performance received rave reviews from discerning critics and educated listeners. His success was so sound that it attracted the attention of James Redpath's Boston Lyceum Bureau, who signed him up for their regular circuit and promoted him as one of their keynote speakers.

Sam soon found that in the post–Civil War lyceum era, lecturing was an easy and quick way to make money for someone like him who had a gift for telling a story. The country had just been through a horrible ordeal with the war and was ripe, if not downright needy, for humorists. Clemens made money at lecturing before he made any money at all publishing books. His notoriety as a lecturer ran so closely alongside his writing career that studies of his 30 years on the lecture circuit alone have kept scholars occupied for many years.

From 1866 to 1895, Clemens delivered nearly 1,000 lectures and speeches, giving over 200 lectures in the United States and Canada alone. Overall, he embarked on 7 major tours in 30 years. He performed in 23 states and several countries around the world. During his world tour in 1895, he spent 8 weeks in Australia, 6 in New Zealand, 8 weeks in India, and 7 in South Africa besides giving lectures in Europe and North America. His last tour opened in Cleveland, Ohio, on July 15, 1895, and closed in London in May of 1896 when the then famous author was over 60 years old.

The lecture circuit was long and arduous. In the 1871–72 season when Clemens took to the circuit soon after his marriage to Livy Langdon, he gave 76 lectures in 15 states and Washington, D.C. He earned approximately $100 to $150 per lecture, but kept barely 15 percent of this amount to bring home to his family after expenses. After many years on the tour, Clemens became in demand and stopped in so many towns and villages that the early days of stage fright in San Francisco and New York must have seemed like they happened in another lifetime.

Clemens was known for several techniques in lecturing that became his trademark. One was that he artfully blended humor with something vital to say, such as commentary on the human condition or the current state of affairs in the country, or information about places he had seen that his audience might find new or exotic. Another was his perfectly straight-faced, dead-pan humor that complimented the well-pitched, low Kentucky drawl he'd inherited from his mother. One reviewer claimed that Clemens (he was known as Mark Twain on his lecture tours as well as for his books) took one minute to say three words. He was not afraid to use the pause in his delivery and became the master of the well-timed and excruciatingly long tests of a pause with an audience. He knew how to read an audience and was quick on his feet to make changes when necessary or beneficial for the effect he wanted. Comics of today would say Mark Twain's "timing" was impeccable.

His entrances became notorious. Often he refused to be introduced and came out on stage and introduced himself. Other times the spotlight would find him sitting at the piano where he'd look up, seemingly surprised to see the audience gathered there. Still other times he walked out on the stage, walked around the podium, came back and leaned on it, then just stared at the audience without saying a word. Pretty soon, this staring made someone in the audience uncomfortable enough to laugh, and one laugh brought another and yet another until he had the whole audience in tune with him without yet uttering a word. He often said that if one could do that, the rest of the evening was easy.

Clemens found long tours on the road exhilarating but exhausting at the same time. Often the hosts of the event kept him up long hours afterward out socializing, which would not bother him in principle most of the time, but given the tight travel schedules of most of his tours, became taxing on his energies. Others wanted to meet him early in the morning, which would set him in a particularly foul mood for the rest of the day. The food and accommodations at the different venues were uneven, often poor. While he was a single man making money, these factors played less of a part, but once Sam became a family man with a wife and children that tours were taking him away from, his patience for these and other inconveniences wore thin.

In later tours when his audience was assured and he was making good money for all concerned with the tour and not just for himself, Clemens placed several demands on James Redpath in scheduling a tour to ease the rigors of endless travel and time away from his family. He wanted lectures to be scheduled along main train routes; he wanted to stay in the finest hotels; he would go no further west than St. Louis (his family by then was living in Hartford, Connecticut). Because of bad memories or disagreements with management at the lecture facilities in these towns or for some other reason, he refused to lecture in Buffalo or Jamestown, New York. He also refused to give any lectures in a church.

Though lectures are a different literary performance art than readings, after he began publishing widely, Clemens began to incorporate elements of both in his presentations. If he were asked to give a reading, for example, he often abandoned the text after awhile and adlibbed humorous anecdotes. If he were giving an informative lecture, sometimes a reading from his own or others' works would be incorporated as part of it.

In his book, *The Trouble Begins at Eight: Mark Twain's Lecture Tours*, Fred W. Lorch indicates that eventually Clemens turned from lectures to readings in his performance career. Sometimes after he left a lecture venue, he found his carefully written and memorized lecture printed in the newspaper, which would leave him angry and with no fresh material to present in the next city. Lectures, like essays, required that the performer have something to say, a point of some kind to make—information, an argument, or moral stance. It was difficult to write new lectures on the road, and as time went on and many audiences had heard a Mark Twain lecture, Clemens was frequently criticized by reviewers as having nothing more of merit to say, that his lectures were merely a loose excuse for stringing jokes together (this shows the difference in expectation between the lecture circuit of those days and the stand-up comedy routines of today, where audiences expect the comic to string jokes together, one after the other). Readings, on the other hand, allowed Clemens to focus on the jokes and adlibs entirely without having to worry about preparing a lecture with a theme besides. The reading became the theme that held the performance together, and Clemens could add and subtract bits of humor at whim.

Clemens may have given his first professional reading (as opposed to lecture) in Boston in November, 1876, ten years and several published books after his first lecture in San Francisco. The range of his reading audiences was striking. One week he gave a one-hour reading to the literary society at West Point for the United States Military Academy cadets and two weeks later he read at an African church for the black residents of Hartford, where he allowed no whites to be admitted except those who came with him. Lorch contends that Clemens viewed readings of printed material as taking more skill than informative lectures and that the challenge appealed to him to perfect the well-performed reading that Charles Dickens was so famous for doing in Europe and America. Later readings were not limited to his own works such as *Huckleberry Finn*, which he annotated and changed for use on the platform, but they also included stories such as the Uncle Remus tale, "Tar Baby." Books still exist that contain marginalia in Clemens's hand, indicating how he should read certain poems or passages, notes on words to say louder, when to pause, and so forth. Many of his lecture notes are a series of tiny sketches on pieces of paper. He said it was easier to keep up the flow of a lecture or reading by remembering what story to tell next by looking at a picture than reading from a list of notes where one could easily lose one's place.

During his 1895 world tour, Clemens needed a unifying idea that he could alter from place to place but that would give him enough material to make such a magnificent tour worthwhile and would not require completely fresh material at each stop. He hit upon the idea of pretending that the lecture tour had the moral purpose of calling for a rebirth of all humanity to improve morality. The irony was built in from the beginning. In a post-modern way, Clemens made fun of the lecture form as an edifying experience for audiences even as he used that form to pay his debts and entertain his audience at the same time. Readings that had been popular with his audiences years ago were selected and related to the theme. This allowed him to go off on tangents at will and at whim, which he did with a flourish. The theme worked. The tour was immensely popular, and Clemens came home, after 13 grueling months of traveling through several continents, in better financial condition.

All of these trips were ahead of Clemens, however, when he enjoyed his success in San Francisco that first night enough to schedule his first lecture tour through Nevada and California later that year. Between October 11 and December 10, 1866, Clemens presented 16 lectures. In California he spoke in the cities and towns of San Francisco, Petaluma, Oakland, San Jose, Sacramento, Marysville, Grass Valley, Nevada City, You Bet, and Red Dog. In Nevada, he lectured in Washoe City, Carson City, Virginia City, Gold Hill, Dayton, and Silver City. The success of this first tour and the money he earned so quickly from it encouraged him to take on another tour the following spring in Missouri and Iowa.

Back in the early days in Nevada and California, Clemens found a niche in the lecture circuit and in traveling and writing. In December 1866, Clemens left California for good and moved to New York City. There he not only confirmed his lecturing prowess but also began another adventure that took him further away from his humble roots, even further away than the great Amazon River he once tried sailing down the Mississippi to catch a boat to see.

VOYAGE ON *THE QUAKER CITY*

Clemens had a new assignment from the *San Francisco Alta California* to take a trip and send letters back to the paper about what he saw. This time he was to go to the Mediterranean area, the Holy Land, and other exotic places in the East. The steamboat was called the *Quaker City*, and the observations Clemens made on the trip formed the basis for a later book that he called *Innocents Abroad*.

The *Quaker City* Holy Land excursion was initiated by Henry Ward Beecher, then minister of a church in Brooklyn. It was the first transatlantic cruise organized in history simply for pleasure. Beecher played up the cruise as a pilgrimage of the Christian faithful to see the Holy Land and also advocated its educational value. Tickets were not cheap—$1,250 per passenger. Most of those who bought them were well-to-do, devout Protestants in their middle age. Of the 65 to 70 passengers on the voyage, only 17 of them were women, and only four of these were unmarried. Entertainment on the boat during the long journey across the ocean consisted of shuffle board, cards, a dance once in awhile, and prayer meetings.

Into this quiet group of wealthy travelers the *Alta* inserted its 31-year-old reporter, Mark Twain. The boat launched from New York on June 8, 1867, and endured several days of rough crossing; most of the passengers got seasick, with the exception of Sam Clemens, who had achieved his sea legs in recent sailings to Hawaii, Nicaragua, and New York. The ship finally reached Gibraltar on June 29. Passengers left and rejoined the ship at various points along the Mediterranean, so the ship and Clemens's travels did not exactly coincide. On the trip, pilgrims visited Spain, Marseilles, Paris, Genoa, Naples, Switzerland, Greece, Constantinople, Yalta, Smyrna, Ephesus, Beirut, Jaffa, Egypt, and Algiers, among other places. The trip lasted 164 days. Passengers spent 46 of those days on the Atlantic Ocean, and 118 sailing the Mediterranean and Black Seas. The *Quaker City* returned to New York on November 19, 1867.

Sam Clemens spent more than half of the days of the voyage, some 98, on the boat itself, much of the time in his cabin writing. The theme of this voyage for him seemed to be that Americans need not bow down in reverence to the ancient antiquities of Europe, the Holy Land, and the East. He poked fun at most of the sights he wrote about, though some he praised, and found as much to ridicule about his fellow Americans' behavior on the trip as he did the sights. Two years later, *The Innocents Abroad, or The New Pilgrims' Progress; Being Some Account of the Steamship Quaker City's Pleasure Excursion to Europe and the Holy Land*, was published in 1869. Other than the jumping frog story and accompanying sketches that Webb printed for him earlier, *Innocents Abroad* became Samuel Clemens's first published book.

The voyage was not all a negative experience for the restless Clemens. He made at least two valuable friends on the ship. One was Mary Mason Fairbanks and the other was Charles Langdon. Mrs. Fairbanks was a former schoolteacher who was married to Abel Fairbanks, who was the owner and editor of the *Cleveland Herald*. She traveled on the *Quaker City* alone, and her knowledge of French and ability to help otherwise communicate gave her a maternal role on the ship for a group of the passengers. Clemens later called her "Mother Fairbanks," though she was only seven years older than he was. Sam and Mary hit it off aboard the ship, though they apparently did not travel much ashore together. Mary wrote several travel letters as well while on the voyage and sent them to her husband's newspaper, where they were published under the pseudonym "Myra." Some scholars believe Fairbanks may have helped Clemens edit his letters into the book manuscript for *Innocents Abroad,* but evidence of this remains sketchy. After the journey, Sam and Mary remained close; they corresponded and kept up with each other's lives for 30 years.

The other important friend Sam Clemens made aboard the *Quaker City* was Charles Jervis Langdon. Charley was the 17-year-old only son of wealthy Jervis and Olivia Langdon of Elmira, New York. Jervis Langdon had made his money in the coal business, and as the only son, Charley was expected to take it over some day. The trip was no doubt an effort at providing the heir apparent with a more worldly education.

Charley fell in with "Mother" Fairbanks and her circle on the *Quaker City* and apparently became fascinated with the Western ruffian onboard. How Clemens initially felt about young Charley's attention is debated; some think he found the cultured gentleman's interest annoying, claiming that he may have been the model for the "Interrogation Point" in *Innocents Abroad.*

Years later, however, Sam related many times an event on the trip with Charley Langdon that changed his life forever. As he tells it, the ship was somewhere in the Bay of Smyrna when, in Charley's cabin, the young man showed Sam a miniature portrait on ivory of his sister, Olivia. Sam claims to have fallen in love at once. Livy, as she was commonly called, was 10 years younger than Sam almost to the day and was Charley's older sister. Immediately on seeing her picture, Sam began plotting with Charley on when and how they might meet. In a single instant, Charley Langdon became a more interesting young man to know in the view of Samuel Clemens.

LIVY LANGDON

Charley kept his word to help Sam meet his sister when their voyage overseas was over. The *Quaker City* passengers and their families had a reunion in New York City in December of 1867, and Sam attended with the primary hope of meeting Charley's family, one member of it in particular.

As Sam describes it in his autobiography, he called at the St. Nicholas Hotel where the Langdons were staying and that is where he met Livy. From that day on for the rest of his life, she never left his thoughts. Fortuitously, he accompanied her to a reading given by Charles Dickens at Steinway Hall on December 31, 1867. Dickens's performance made an impression on the young lecturer. The famous British author wore a black velvet suit with a bright red flower pinned to his lapel. Spotlights highlighted his presence and defined his features just like a prized painting on a wall in contrast with the half-darkened audience. That night he read from *David Copperfield*. Dickens not only read from his books, but he performed them as well, reading with such passion and energy that his audience was greatly moved.

Sam and Livy's "first date" is interesting in that it set their relationship in a literary context right from the start. Literature was something both of them enjoyed and came to share with each other. Much of their correspondence talks about books they have read or recommend to each other. Livy's good editing sense contributed much to Sam's later writing for publication; in fact, she would become the chief editor of his work and the one he trusted most to comment on it accurately and fairly.

The courtship of Sam Clemens and Livy Langdon was performed primarily through correspondence and Sam's short visits to Elmira. Sam wrote Livy 184 letters over the course of their two-year courtship. On one visit, Sam managed through Charley Langdon to stay for a week. The week came to an end and about eight or nine o'clock on a cold winter's evening, Sam reluctantly boarded a wagon outside the Langdon home to head for New York City. Charley lit a cigar and joined him on the back seat that was set there temporarily and not securely fastened. The two men waved at the family gathered to say good-bye on the Langdon front porch. Barney, the coachman, touched the horse with his whip to start them off, and the horse sprang forward so quickly that the seat dislodged and Charley and Sam fell off. Sam's head hit the ice so hard that it knocked him out—or at least that was the story.

Sam was able to extend his visit at the Langdon's by three more days and enjoy the solicitude of not only Livy's sister, Susan Crane and her husband, Theodore, but also the family physician (who proclaimed there were no bumps or bruises, and that a good night's rest should be sufficient for the "patient," though the patient disagreed and would not proclaim himself recovered in the morning). Best of all, Sam enjoyed the comforting nursing care of Livy herself and the two fell more in love as Sam made plain to her that he believed he needed her in his life, and she began to realize that "reforming" this ruffian with her more refined ways might be just what the doctor ordered for her own happiness.

On the next visit to Elmira, Sam proposed. Livy had refused previous proposals from him, but Sam had been persistent. This time, she agreed but only if he obtained her father's approval of the marriage. Jervis Langdon saw that his daughter loved Sam and knew Sam fairly well by this time from his frequent visits to Elmira and his friendship with Charley and the family. Despite his wealth, Langdon was a generous, forward-thinking man, an abolitionist who had hidden escaped slaves in his home as part of the Underground Railroad. He was friends with Frederick Douglass. Even though he believed he knew Sam, he was concerned that Sam had appeared in their lives in New York and Elmira out of context of any family or background. Charley was too young to have his high regard for Clemens be the only reference for him to become a member of the family. Jervis agreed to accept the engagement provisionally on obtaining character references from other people Sam knew. Until then, all must keep the engagement a secret. Sam provided Mr. Langdon with the names and addresses of six prominent people in San Francisco, two of them clergymen. Langdon said they would speak of the matter no more until he had had a chance to write to these people and receive their replies.

Some time later, Mr. Langdon summoned Sam to a private meeting. He had received the replies to his letters, and he read Sam every one. The letters were not only unfavorable, they were damning. No one recommended him. More than one said that Clemens would end up in a drunkard's grave. Another went so far as to say that not only would he never allow any daughter of his to marry Sam Clemens, but he would rather see her dead than married to him! After Mr. Langdon finished reading, there was a pause, and he asked Sam if he didn't know anyone who would speak favorably on his behalf. "Haven't you a friend in the world?" he asked. Clemens replied that it was apparently not the case. Then "I'll be your friend myself," Langdon said. "Take the girl. I know you better than they do."[5]

Later on, Langdon heard Sam speak fondly and enthusiastically of Joe Goodman and commented that he seemed to be a friend of Sam's. Why hadn't Sam given him his name when Langdon asked for references? Sam replied that he knew Mr. Langdon wanted honest appraisals and that Goodman would have been too complimentary on the other side. He expected honesty on the part of those whose names he did provide, but he did not expect them to be as negative as they turned out to be.

This was how Sam Clemens and Livy Langdon came to be officially engaged on February 4, 1869. Sam gave his love a solid gold ring with the date inscribed on the inside. While his relationship with Livy did not end his travels by any means, it did provide him, finally, with a home territory for his heart, no matter where they lived, where they roamed, or what troubles or joys befell them.

NOTES

1. Mark Twain, *Life on the Mississippi* (Boston: James R. Osgood, 1883), chap. 21.

2. Mark Twain, *Roughing It*, ed. Harriet Elinor Smith, Edgar Marquess Branch, Lin Salamo, and Robert Pack Browning (Berkeley: University of California Press, 1995), chap. 1.

3. Charles Neider, ed., *The Autobiography of Mark Twain, Including Chapters Now Published for the First Time* (New York: Harper & Row, 1959), p. 200.

4. Neider, *Autobiography*, p. 200.

5. Neider, *Autobiography*, p. 248.

Chapter 5

THE GILDED YEARS: 1870–1889

After meeting and courting Olivia Langdon, Sam Clemens was about to embark on the happiest and most productive years of his life. Similarly to the phrase he coined with his co-author C. D. Warner, "the Gilded Age," in his 1873 novel, *The Gilded Age: A Tale of To-day*, the years from the day of his marriage to Livy to the end of the century were particularly fruitful and golden for Clemens, both personally and professionally. Though they were not without trouble or tragedy, they were truly the gilded years of his life.

BUFFALO

Sam and Livy were married in the parlor of the Langdon home in Elmira, New York, on February 2, 1870. The ceremony was co-officiated by Rev. Thomas Beecher, pastor of Park Church in Elmira where the Langdons attended services and Joseph Twichell of Hartford, who was a friend of Sam's. Sam's sister and niece, Pamela and Annie Moffett, made the trip to the wedding but Jane and Orion Clemens stayed in Missouri. Clemens's mother promised she would be the first visitor to the new couple's home in the spring. Mary Fairbanks from the *Quaker City* and a few other friends also attended. In preparation, Sam took the golden engagement ring from Livy and had it engraved with the date of their wedding. He claimed later that from that day on, Livy never took it off for any reason.

Where the new couple was to live after the wedding was a cause of some concern for Sam. Jervis Langdon gave Sam money to buy a share in the *Buffalo Express*. He gave the money as a gift, an advance on Livy's inheritance, but Sam thought of it as a loan and intended to pay back every penny. Sam wrote a few pieces for the paper, but he knew nothing about Buffalo, and made a few trips there in preparation for the wedding to find a suitable boardinghouse where he and his new bride could live. He felt that if they boarded for one year, they might save enough money to buy their own home after that.

Right before the wedding in February, Sam made another trip to Buffalo to locate housing. There was some confusion over arrangements he had made with someone who was to help him locate a boardinghouse, and before he knew it, he had to leave without seeing where they would live. He felt uneasy that the house that would be located for them in his absence would be unsatisfactory. During his courtship with Livy, Sam had settled in Hartford, Connecticut, in order to work more closely with his editor on *The Innocents Abroad* and also to be closer to the publishers of New York. Livy helped him edit the manuscript during their engagement. The ownership of the *Buffalo Express* gave him a steady job to begin their married life, while at the same time allowing him to continue to write articles and books.

The couple spent their wedding night in the Langdon home and left the next day for Buffalo. Helping them move Livy's belongings and the couple's wedding gifts to their new home, the Langdons, Pamela Moffett, and a few friends went to Buffalo with them. Once they arrived in town, Sam and Livy were delayed while the rest of the party went on to another location. The driver took Sam and Livy around the block a few times, and soon they were heading down Delaware Avenue, one of the most prestigious residential streets in the city. When the driver pulled up in front of a splendid house at 472 Delaware Avenue, Clemens became concerned and told him that this house was too elaborate to be a boardinghouse and there must be some mistake. Livy escorted Sam to the door, and when it opened, Jervis Langdon handed the groom the keys to his own home, fully furnished and staffed, as a wedding gift. The astonished and grateful Sam Clemens never had to live in a boardinghouse again. He and Livy began their lives together without financial worry.

The marriage and move into the new house had a profound effect on Sam. While he had been working on and off at a life of letters for several years by this time, he had had no responsibilities to anyone but himself, and he had never held or kept a regular job with regular office hours. The lifestyle of an upper-middle-class literary man, which Jervis Langdon had set up for him, was something he would have to work to maintain and grow into to feel comfortable, and Clemens at that moment must have wondered if that was even possible for him to do.

At the time, the house cost Langdon $40,000, which is equivalent to $800,000 in early twenty-first century money, and the staff included a maid, housekeeper, cook, and coachman. Clemens was not yet used to the change. He had spent years going from job to job and whim to whim wherever the winds may carry him. Gaining this level of responsibility and climb in social status in one fell swoop was a jolt, so in the early days he hid out from his duties at the *Buffalo Express* by having an extended honeymoon with Livy in the house. The young woman whose family once thought she might not marry because of her frail health enjoyed a healthy and satisfying romantic life with her new husband, and he with her.

Clemens wrote to an old friend, "I have at this moment the only sweetheart I ever loved, & bless her old heart she is lying asleep upstairs in a bed that I sleep in every night, & for four whole days she has been Mrs. Samuel L. Clemens!"[1] For her part, Livy was also joyously happy. She wrote that when Ellen, the housemaid she'd brought from Elmira, once asked her if she were homesick, she replied, "no . . . I [am] as happy as a queen."[2] Within a few short weeks she was pregnant with their first child, and Sam's overload of responsibility became even heavier.

He had written several pieces for the *Buffalo Express* in the months leading up to his marriage, some 50 in fact, but in the first few months after the wedding he wrote only 15. Not only was his adjustment to his new life distracting (he became obsessed at one point with the buttons on the coachman's coat and complained that the coat cost more than any coat he had ever worn himself), but he also had good royalties coming in from *Innocents Abroad* to take his attention away from newspaper work and more toward the writing of books and the life he had left behind in Hartford. The American Publishing Company was there as were friends he'd made, Isabella Hooker and Joe Twichell. They were campaigning to bring him back to Hartford in such a public way that at one point Clemens had to issue a public denial in the *Buffalo Express* that he was leaving the area.

That summer, the first trouble of a string of them that would occur in their first year of marriage struck the Clemenses. Jervis Langdon became deathly ill, and Sam and Livy were summoned to his bedside in Elmira. They stayed several weeks while Jervis's health continued to deteriorate. On August 6, 1870, the benefactor and father figure to Samuel Clemens died. "Father died this afternoon," he telegraphed to his mother and sister.[3] With his father-in-law's death, Sam must have felt the burden of responsibility weigh even more heavily—gone was the man he could count on to help him with these new burdens if he needed it.

Langdon's estate was worth approximately $1 million and was divided equally among his wife, his son Charley, and daughter Livy. Susan Crane was an adopted daughter, and to her, Langdon left a piece of property he owned on East Hill in Elmira called Quarry Farm.

Livy was devastated at her father's death. Pregnant and of ill-physical health anyway, Livy gave Sam even more reason to worry about her and her condition. They returned to Buffalo in late August, but the house no longer was a happy one. It kept reminding them of Jervis Langdon and his generosity. Sam threw himself into his work, beginning a new book, *Roughing It*. Livy's mother came to stay with them and help Livy run the household, and an old friend of Livy's, Emma Nye, also came to help keep her company while Sam was trying to write.

While with them in Buffalo, Emma Nye became ill with what turned out to be typhoid fever, so the Clemenses soon had another sick person to care for. They gave Emma their bed and Livy sat at her side night after night, at times not even changing her clothes. By the end of September, Emma died. Another friend, Mary Fairbanks, paid a visit to the Clemenses, and when she left, Livy got into the carriage to escort her to the train station. The coachman, Patrick, was in such a hurry to make the train, that he ran the horse out in full gallop, and Livy was bumped and thrown so much in the carriage that a miscarriage became imminent and the doctor put her on bed rest. Sam wrote Orion that he had moved her bed downstairs to the library where he could help keep careful watch until her due date in December.

During these early months of their marriage, Sam's family had moved from Missouri to the East. Whether it was to be closer to Sam or not is unclear, but Jane Clemens, his mother, and Pamela Moffett, his sister, moved to nearby Fredonia, New York. Pamela often visited the Clemenses, and she was there in November. Susan Crane, Livy's adopted sister, was also there to help. Susan was a very generous and giving woman, much like Jervis Langdon, and Sam came to accept and enjoy her company as much as Livy did. Both Pamela and Susan were there in early November when Livy suddenly went into labor.

On November 7, 1870, Langdon Clemens was born prematurely, weighing only four and one-half pounds. He was not expected to live. Livy's health deteriorated after the birth until she came down with typhoid fever. Dr. Rachel Brooks Gleason, who with her husband, Dr. Silas O. Gleason, ran a water cure in Elmira and were the Langdon family physicians, was summoned to Buffalo to treat Livy. Sam claims he did not allow the doctor to leave the house until Livy was securely on the mend.

A wet nurse was hired to help with the baby, who managed to gain some weight but seemed to cry day and night. The man who had loved the freedom of his life as a steamboat pilot gliding down the Mississippi must have wondered whether he had sold his soul to the devil for the curse of troubles that piled up in that house in Buffalo in so short a time. Not able to make money to support his family and household unless he could write and not able to write without the ability to concentrate and focus, his frustration grew until he wrote to Elisha Bliss, his publisher, "if that baby goes on crying 3 more hours this way I will butt my frantic brains out & try to get some peace."[4]

By March 1871, Clemens believed he needed to get himself and his family out of Buffalo as quickly as possible and make a fresh start. He had managed to repay much of his father-in-law's loan, and the royalties from *Innocents Abroad* were still coming in. His publisher and friends in Hartford were still asking him to move there. Hartford was where his work really was, since his royalty checks came from there, and the success of the book had made Bliss also express interest in publishing *Roughing It*. He put up the wedding-gift house for sale at an asking price of $25,000; that did not include the furnishings. He also sold his $25,000 share of the *Buffalo Express* to one of his partners for a $1,000-down payment and the rest to be paid over the next five years. Clemens was cutting his losses in more ways than one. He told friends that he would not use his wife's inheritance to pay the bills, but he would use it for special purchases and needs. He wrote to Orion, "We . . . are going to spend the summer in Elmira while we build a house in Hartford. Eight months' sickness & death in one place is enough for Yrs. Truly."[5] The Hartford house would give the Clemenses the new start they sought. Its extravagance, however, under Clemens's ill-trained flair for handling money would also bring them troubles of a different kind.

QUARRY FARM

Right after their disastrous first year in Buffalo but before their move to Connecticut, Sam and Livy stayed at the summer home of the Langdons on East Hill above Elmira called Quarry Farm. The spot would rescue the Clemenses' spirits many times over the next 20 years and became the location where Sam began many of the masterpieces for which he is so well known today. Since the house and grounds of Quarry Farm remained under the private ownership of the Langdon family until 1983, research into the farm and its importance in the author's life and work has only become more developed in the last two decades.

The land that would become Quarry Farm began as 287 acres owned in 1788 by Cornelius Roberts. In the early nineteenth century, Roberts sold it to merchant and land dealer, Robert Cowell. In the middle of the nineteenth century, farmer and mason John Henry Faustnaught purchased 37.5 acres of the holding and set up a quarry on the property. In 1869,

Faustnaught sold 7 acres, a few outbuildings, and a stonecutter's cottage to Jervis Langdon for $3,553.12.

Jervis Langdon apparently expanded the stonecutter's cottage a bit, making it so that his family and perhaps one servant could stay summer weekends there in some comfort. The house was still not large. Langdon's friend and neighbor on East Hill, Rev. Thomas K. Beecher, named the property Quarry Farm after the abandoned quarry at the site. Other neighbors included Drs. Silas O. and Rachel Brooks Gleason, who owned and managed the well-known water cure on East Hill.

When Jervis Langdon died in 1870, Quarry Farm was bequeathed to his eldest child, Susan Langdon Crane. She and her husband, Theodore, expanded the house further and eventually made the farm their permanent home in 1886. Under the Cranes' ownership, the property developed to contain a large house done in the style of Andrew Jackson Downing's "Bracketed Cottage, with Veranda," from his *Architecture of Country Houses*. The veranda began as a narrow, vine-covered arbor but was eventually widened. The slats of the arbor were filled in to form the "architectural veranda" style with a roof. A wooden floor to the veranda was covered with oriental rugs, and large, wide shades could be rolled down the sides of the porch to protect it from wind or rain. One large parlor window could be opened completely, much like a larger version of patio doors today, to extend the parlor out onto the porch. Much after the time of the Cranes and Clemenses, the wooden floors of the veranda were replaced by slate in the 1950s.

The porch framed and commanded a west view of the Chemung River and the city of Elmira below, backdropped by rolling hills that led into Pennsylvania. This view is striking and alluring, even today.

In the summer of 1871, Susan and Theodore Crane invited Sam and Livy Clemens to visit them at Quarry Farm for the summer. This summer visit initiated a nearly annual ritual for the author and his family. They "removed" to the farm each summer for nearly 20 years, from 1871 to 1889 and then again in 1895 and 1903. Since Livy preferred going home to her mother's and sister's care during the last days of her pregnancies, all three of the Clemens daughters were born at Quarry Farm as well.

In 1874, Susan Crane, whose calm temperament and generous spirit enjoyed the less than predictable ways of her sister's husband, surprised him with a gift when the family arrived at the farm that year. She had commissioned the construction of an octagonal study just for her brother-in-law to work in on a crest about 100 yards above the farmhouse. The study overlooked the valley below and was far enough way from the main house that the author could have peace and quiet. Clemens not only loved the generous and thoughtful gift, but he managed to begin working there immediately and found in the solitude and natural surroundings an environment greatly conducive to his productivity.

The study contained eight pocket windows that could slide up into the wall above and create an open-air pavilion if the author so desired. It had a fireplace with a split chimney so that a window fit in that wall. Furniture rotated from the house to the study and back in different summers and times during each summer, depending on what the author wanted. There was a rug on the floor, a small table, and books. At times, Clemens had a bed in it, as well.

Twain described his study this way:

> It is the loveliest study you ever saw. It is . . . a cosy nest, and just room in it for a sofa, table and three or four chairs, and when the storm sweeps down the remote valley, and the lightning flashes behind the hills beyond, and the rain beats on the roof over my head, imagine the luxury of it."[6]

Over the years at Quarry Farm, Clemens began work and continued it on several books, including titles now considered his masterpieces. *The Adventures of Tom Sawyer* was likely conceived at Quarry Farm. While his children laughed and played in their playhouse, "Ellerslie," on the grounds below the study on lazy summer afternoons, the author looked out over the river valley and hills beyond from the quiet of his "cosy nest" and let his thoughts drift back to Hannibal, Missouri, the great Mississippi, Cardiff Hill and Lover's Leap, and his own boyhood. He started the manuscript for *Adventures of Huckleberry Finn* at Quarry Farm as well, editing as he went. One can only envision that the quiet of the hillside allowed him to hear and capture the voices of Huck and Jim more clearly, as revisions appearing in the original manuscript attest.

In an 1883 letter to William Dean Howells, he wrote:

> I haven't piled up manuscript so in years as I have done since we came here to the farm three weeks and a half ago. I wrote four thousand words today and I touch three thousand and upward pretty often, and don't fall below twenty-six hundred any working day. And when I get fagged out, I like abed a couple of days and read and smoke, and then go it again for six or seven days. The book I half-finished two or three years ago I expect to complete in a months or so . . . two months more. And I shall like it whether anybody else does or not.[7]

The book he was referring to in the letter was *Adventures of Huckleberry Finn*. Other titles known to have been worked on at the farm are: *Rough-*

ing It, A Tramp Abroad, The Prince and the Pauper, Life on the Mississippi, and *A Connecticut Yankee in King Arthur's Court.*

The farm provided a respite from the social responsibilities and events the Clemenses were obliged to perform at their mansion in Hartford, Connecticut, and, one might say, provided the author with a visceral connection to the country living of his youth and summers spent with family and stories at the Quarleses' farm (even the names of the farms are similar). His typical day was to climb the stone steps up the hill to the study around ten each morning. He skipped lunch and worked until dinnertime. After dinner, he often shared what he had written with his appreciative family sitting around him on the veranda. Reading the manuscript aloud was an important part of Clemens's creative process. Livy and the girls made comments on the manuscript in progress quite frequently, the girls often wanting to keep passages that Livy found too strained. Sam took to writing flamboyant passages on purpose into his manuscript that he knew would bring this rise out of his daughters in that evening's reading, just so that he could enjoy seeing their reaction when their mother, soon catching on but playing along, recommended that the passages be cut.

The years at Quarry Farm were among the happiest of not only Sam Clemens's life but also the lives of the entire Clemens, Langdon, and Crane families.

HARTFORD

Though Sam Clemens took his father-in-law's offer to begin his married life in Buffalo, New York, and he found peace and quiet in which to work at Quarry Farm in Elmira, it was Hartford, Connecticut, where Sam Clemens chose on his own to build a house and settle with his family. His publisher and editor were there; Hartford had a growing scene of writers and cultural life, and the city was halfway between the publishing capital of the United States in New York City and the New England capital of Boston. Clemens made Hartford his home for two decades, longer than any other single address, though about a third of that time he spent away from the city on lecture tours, working at Quarry Farm, or traveling in Europe.

Clemens tried to purchase the *Hartford Courant* before marrying Livy, but the publisher, J. R. Hawley, would not sell it. Eventually, Clemens created his own publishing company in the city, Charles L. Webster & Company. The Hartford years marked a time of extraordinary success and happiness in Clemens's personal and professional life, though they were not without some difficulties.

After they left Buffalo in the summer of 1871 and recuperated for a time from their traumatic first year of marriage by spending time with the Langdons and Cranes in Elmira and at Quarry Farm, the Clemenses rented a house on Forest Street in Hartford. The house was owned by Isabella Beecher Hooker, sister of Harriet Beecher Stowe and Thomas Ward Beecher and a friend of Olivia Lewis Langdon, Sam's mother-in-law. The house was in the west section of Hartford where several writers and publishers lived, including Harriet Beecher Stowe, famous author of *Uncle Tom's Cabin*. The area was known as Nook Farm. Sam wanted to build their new house in the Nook Farm area as well. They lived at the Forest Street house. Soon the whole community watched as the large and eccentric structure they commissioned was constructed.

While living at the Forest Street house, the Clemenses enjoyed success and suffered a tragic loss. On March 19, 1872, Olivia Susan (Susy) Clemens was born in Elmira. The Clemenses named her after her mother (and grandmother, whose name was also Olivia) and her aunt Susan Crane. They took the new baby back to Hartford. Clemens now had a son and a daughter. Also that year, his book *Roughing It* was published by the American Publishing Company. Clemens's lively account of his adventures in Nevada and California was selling well.

Tragedy struck when little Langdon died on June 2, 1872, just two and a half months after Susy (as they called her) was born. Though Langdon had been born prematurely and suffered from colds and ailments all of his short life, Sam blamed himself for his death. Langdon died from diphtheria, but Sam never forgave himself for the day he took Langdon outside and allowed the blanket to slip off of him in cold weather. His guilt over this latest tragedy echoed his feelings over previous family deaths, from his sister Margaret in his childhood, to his brother Henry in his young adulthood on the river. Clemens never seemed to get over the feeling that he could have done something to save the loved ones he lost. Langdon, just 19 months old, their firstborn, and the only son Sam and Livy would ever have, was buried in the Langdon family plot at Woodlawn Cemetery in Elmira.

In 1873, for $31,000, Sam and Livy bought five acres of land at 372 Farmington Avenue, next door to Harriet Beecher Stowe, and hired a New York City architect, Edward Tuckerman Potter, to design a house. Potter was known for his originality and designed mostly churches and college buildings but he had just finished a home for George Warner, whose brother C. D. Warner would later work with Clemens on his first novel, *The Gilded Age*. Working with Livy's sketches, Potter designed a 3-story, 18-room brick and wood house overlooking a picturesque bend in the Park River and the surrounding countryside. The house included Gothic turrets and an octagonal pilothouse-sort-of room that caused observers later on to call it a "Steamboat Gothic" design. When it was completed, it became known as the most unusual home not only in Hartford but in all of Connecticut. Potter oversaw the building of the house, which was finished in September or October of 1874 and cost the Clemenses $70,000. They spent $21,000 on furniture.

The Clemenses had spent so much money on the exterior of the house that they had to move in with the interior yet unfinished. Sam and Livy had another baby that summer, Clara Langdon Clemens, born in Elmira on June 8, so the family who moved in the large home at the end of the year consisted of Sam and Livy and their two daughters.

They had used Livy's inheritance to build the house, but now finishing the interior the way the house demanded required more money. As he had done before, Clemens hit the lecture circuit to earn quick cash. That and the success of *The Adventures of Tom Sawyer,* which was published in 1876, allowed the Clemenses to go back to work on completing the house in 1881. They hired Louis Comfort Tiffany's design company, Associated Artists, to decorate the first floor. Today, the Mark Twain House in Hartford is open as a museum, and the downstairs is one of only two remaining Tiffany-decorated interiors open to the public.

The entrance hall is impressive with an ornate stairway carved by Leon Marcotte of Paris and New York. Tiffany's company stenciled silver on the original paneling and hand-painted the ceiling and walls red with blue patterns. A large Tiffany window once refracted light entering the room but it has since been removed. Sidelight glass windows of lilies remain. The drawing room, where guests were entertained formally, was decorated in silver East Indian designs over salmon pink, and was designed by Lockwood de Forest, a Tiffany partner at Associated Artists. A large mirror in the room came to the house from the Clemenses' days in Buffalo. It was originally a wedding gift.

Continuing on the first floor, visitors entered the dining room where elaborate dinner parties were held, then continued on to the library, where the first object that would have drawn their attention was not books but the huge mantelpiece over the fireplace. Clemens read from his work at the fire, told his family and friends stories, and occasionally recited poetry there. He purchased the mantelpiece in Europe where it had originally belonged to the Mitchell-Innes family who commissioned its carving, which included their family crest. The mantelpiece originally stood in the dining room of Ayles Castle in Scotland. It is as wide as the fireplace and rises all the way up from there to the ceiling. In fact, the original mantel was so tall that the Clemenses had to cut off the very top of it and mount that section elsewhere in the room over a doorway.

As his daughters grew, Sam liked to tell them stories in front of the fire. Knickknacks such as vases, plates, and paintings on the mantel became part of the stories, and the girls insisted he use them each night in a new story but in exactly the same order. The story always had to begin with the painting of "The Cat in the Ruff" at one end and finish with the painting of the young woman they named "Emmeline" that hung on the wall at the opposite side of the mantel. Clemens claimed that the objects began to show "wear" after all the violence they survived from night after night of wild and bloody adventures.

At one end of the library is a windowed conservatory that catches the light and offers what used to be views down the hill to the river but city development has made these views from the house no longer visible. Plants still grow well in the bright alcove. Another alcove in the large library was where the children sat and read. The children were well accommodated in the mansion and given their special places. Small furniture the girls used when they were young still exists in the house.

The second floor of the Hartford house had a room that used to be Sam's study. Once the girls became school-aged, however, Sam moved out of the room in order to allow the children to use it as a classroom, since they were tutored at home. The second floor was also where Sam and Livy's bedroom was located. The Clemens bed, like the ornate mantelpiece, also showed Sam's preference for fancy ornamentation that might appear gaudy to others. The four large posts rise in twisted wood from each corner and are each topped by a large carved angel that can be removed. The Clemens daughters frequently removed them in their play and were allowed to do so.

The headboard was tall as well and carved in large angel designs, as was the smaller footboard. Sam slept with his head at the footboard end of the bed, since he said the headboard was too elaborate not to be able to see it. Sam often smoked cigars and wrote in bed as well and in later years even allowed reporters in his room to interview him as he did so. It is actions like these that allow observers a peek into the character not only of Samuel Clemens once he reached his period of greatest success but also the patience Livy Clemens must have had with her husband.

Finally, on the third floor of the house is located Sam's billiard room. Here, he worked when he was at the Hartford house, though the public nature of the house and the level and amount of entertaining the Clemenses did while there often made working there an impossibility. It became Sam's custom to live with his family, work as best he could, entertain friends and business associates, and work on business dealings at the house in Hartford for nine months of the year, then "remove" to Quarry Farm in the summers to get his real writing done. The billiard room had a large table in the center given to him by an admirer. After dinner parties, he took his male guests up to his private domain for a smoke, a drink, and games of billiards that frequently lasted into the wee hours of the morning.

Clemens biographer Albert Bigelow Paine claimed that the man loved to play billiards. He'd play all nightlong, according to Paine, and when his friends had to leave to go home or turn in at a downstairs guest room, they could look back and still see Clemens hitting balls around the table by himself. When he was there alone, he often shot billiards to help himself think. Tucked at one end of this room was his desk where he attempted to work between social engagements, out of the way of the hustle and bustle of the family dwelling space downstairs.

If the house sounds too extravagant for an author's salary to maintain, that was sometimes the case more than others. The Clemenses lived there at the height of Mark Twain's prolific publishing career and popularity. Books published between 1871 and 1891 when Hartford was the Clemens's official address include: *Mark Twain's (Burlesque) Autobiography and First Romance* (1871); *Roughing It* (1872); *Screamers* (1872); *Choice Humorous Works of Mark Twain* (1873); *The Gilded Age: A Tale of To-day* (co-authored with Charles Dudley Warner; 1874); *Number One: Mark Twain's Sketches* (1874); *Sketches New and Old* (1875); *A True Story and the Recent Carnival of Crime* (1877); *Punch, Brothers, Punch! And Other Sketches* (1878); *A Tramp Abroad* (1880); *[Date, 1601] Conversation as It Was by the Social Fireside in the Time of the Tudors* (1880, privately published); *The Prince and the Pauper: A Tale for Young People of All Ages* (1881); *The Stolen White Elephant* (1882); *Life on the Mississippi* (1883); and *A Connecticut Yankee in King Arthur's Court* (1889).

Of course, these were also the years when the two most well-known Mark Twain classics of American literature were published as well, namely: *The Adventures of Tom Sawyer* (1876); and *Adventures of Huckleberry Finn* (1885).

THE ADVENTURES OF TOM SAWYER

The Adventures of Tom Sawyer is Sam Clemens's most autobiographical novel and his first novel written without a co-author (he'd published his first novel, *The Gilded Age*, co-written with Charles Dudley Warner, three years earlier). Part murder mystery, part coming-of-age story, *Tom Sawyer* is the best-selling of all of Mark Twain's books, seconded by *Adventures of Huckleberry Finn*. Many readers of Mark Twain begin with *Tom Sawyer*, and the novel is considered a classic of American literature.

The story concerns a boy who lives in a small town on the Mississippi River and how he and his friend Huck witness a murder. There are five storylines in 35 chapters and 71,500 words. The storylines overlap. One plot concerns Tom's relationship with family and school friends. A second is his relationship with his sweetheart, Becky Thatcher. Chapters 13–17 develop a third storyline of Tom and his friends, Huck and Joe Harper, hiding out on Jackson's Island, playing pirates. The murder Tom and Huck witness in chapter 9 sets up the fourth plot, which culminates in the trial of Muff Potter, and the fifth is a combination of the search for Injun Joe coupled with Tom and Huck's search for treasure and Tom and Becky's experiences in the cave.

Clemens admitted that Petersburg is modeled after Hannibal and that many of the characters in the novel are modeled after actual people he knew when he lived there as a boy. Tom, he admitted, is himself. He borrowed attributes from his mother and her penchant for trying out new cure-alls to fashion Aunt Polly. Much of Tom's brother Sid's character traits came from Sam's younger brother, Henry. Joe Harper is based on his boyhood friend, Will Bowen. Becky Thatcher developed out of Sam's memories of his own childhood sweetheart, Laura Hawkins, and Huck Finn grew out of his imagination and memories of the son of the town drunk, a boy named Tom Blankenship. While the major events of the novel, such as the murder, are fictitious, smaller incidents such as teasing Becky Thatcher are straight out of Sam's boyhood. The cave in Hannibal actually exists.

Idea for pieces of *Tom Sawyer* wrote themselves to the surface in some of Sam's earlier writing. For example, his early Sunday school days appear in essays such as "Examinations Day." In 1868, he wrote a short story that was never published that anticipated the novel he would write many years later. In a February 1870 letter to Will Bowen, Clemens recalls many of their adventures as children.

The book was published in 1876, the year of the nation's centennial, by the American Publishing Company of Hartford, Connecticut. The first edition was illustrated by True Williams. The book was translated into many languages, and has never gone out of print from the first day it appeared on bookshelves. In 1936, it was illustrated by Norman Rockwell. Clemens wrote other books using Tom Sawyer as a character than this one and *Huck Finn*, but neither of them was ever as popular. *Tom Sawyer Abroad* was published in 1894; *Tom Sawyer, Detective* appeared in 1896.

One appeal that has kept the novel in print around the world for so many years is certainly its depiction of childhood in a playful but realistic way. Tom is a lovable character for all of his faults. He craves adventure and excitement, while at the same time needing love and attention. He wants to act and live his own independent life like a pirate but at the same time he does not quite have the maturity yet and knowledge to do so. These are universal features of growing up.

Another appeal is Clemens's accurate portrayal of setting. The small town of Petersburg rings true even to those readers who have never visited Hannibal, Missouri. Those who have gone there after reading the novel perhaps in childhood, find it uncanny how they instantly recognize where they are when walking down Hill Street, facing the river. Somehow, the positioning of the judge's office, Becky Thatcher's house, the cave, and other spots mentioned in the novel shift into their proper places based on what Clemens has told the reader about them.

Critics have argued that despite Clemens starting and stopping the manuscript in the summer of 1874 (manuscript study indicates this may have occurred after chapter 4), and finishing it the next spring and summer, *Tom Sawyer* is Clemens's most successful novel in terms of structure. The congruent threads of Tom versus adults; Tom versus Becky; Tom versus Huck; and Tom versus Injun Joe provide a secure framework on which the various scenes of the story rest and blend. In Clemens's adopting Tom's point of view, his style for this novel breaks from the more stilted style of *The Gilded Age* and provides a bridge to the vernacular he later uses in *Huckleberry Finn*.

As usual, Clemens had a way of cutting to the chase when it came to describing something the rest of the world had observed but was having trouble putting into words. He called *The Adventures of Tom Sawyer* "a hymn put into prose to give it a worldly air."[8] There will never be a literary critic or reader around who can say it better.

ADVENTURES OF HUCKLEBERRY FINN

Many readers wonder if there really is such a thing as a huckleberry. Indeed, the deep blue berry is native to North America, and it is edible. It resembles the blueberry, except that blueberries are softer and contain tiny seeds. The huckleberry is not native to Missouri, where Clemens's novel is set but rather it is found in the eastern region of the United States. In the nineteenth century, a "huckleberry" was also used as a slang term for a person of no importance. Sam Clemens had never seen nor tasted a huckleberry before 1868 when he wrote about it in an article,

"Morality and Huckleberries" for the *San Francisco Alta California*, and describes his first encounter with them.

In the novel, there are only two characters who call Huck by his full first name. One is Miss Watson when she is scolding him in chapters 1 and 4; the other is in chapter 24 when the King uses it. Tom always calls him Huck.

Clemens admits to beginning the novel in Elmira, in his octagonal study overlooking the Chemung River. An examination of the first page of the original manuscript reveals Clemens tuning his ear for the groundbreaking vernacular style the novel would become so known for later. He changes the first sentence of chapter 1 from "You will not know about me..." to "You don't know about me...."[9]

The novel is 112,000 words long and is divided into 43 chapters of varying lengths. The setting begins in St. Petersburg on the Mississippi and ends in Pikesville, about 1,100 miles down the river over and covers about a year's duration in the 1840s. The novel has three distinct sections: the first, chapters 1–11, occur in St. Petersburg or north of it in Illinois when Pap takes Huck there to stay in his cabin. Huck pretends to be dead, escapes, and finds Jim on Jackson's Island. Chapters 12–30 describe Huck and Jim floating down the Mississippi on a raft. This section takes up almost exactly one-half of the novel and includes several adventures onshore. The third major section comprises chapters 31–43 and is set in and around Pikesville. Huck gets rid of the King and the Duke, and Jim is captured. Huck and Tom help Jim escape.

Since its publication in the United States in 1885, *Huck Finn* has sold more than 20 million copies and has been translated into more than 50 different languages. Love it or hate it (the book has readers in both camps), the novel is an American classic.

Huck is certainly Sam Clemens's masterpiece, but it is also his most controversial work. It was banned in the Concord Library in Massachusetts the year it came out because of the wide use of slang and dialect. They labeled it in a newspaper article as "trash." It is banned in some public-school libraries by school boards even today mostly because of its frequent use of a single racial epithet, commonly called in today's vernacular the "n-word."

The book addresses the question of race in America head-on. Those who love the novel see Clemens dealing with a protagonist who is brought up in a racist, pre–Civil War society who does not see black people as human beings but who slowly, as he makes his way down the heartline of America's Mississippi River, comes to know and see his black friend Jim as a man. Those who hate the novel dislike it for its racial epithets (which proponents argue are there because they were used in the period, and Clemens is portraying things as they were then), and for what they see as stereotyped treatments of African Americans (fans of the novel argue that the stereotypes are part of Clemens's use of satire). The novel has been a lightning rod for emotions on many sides of the racial issue in the United States for over 100 years. In *Green Hills of Africa*, twentieth-century author Ernest Hemingway wrote, "All modern American literature comes from one book by Mark Twain called *Huckleberry Finn*." Black writer David Bradley says that the novel should be taught not only to whites as a novel about race but to blacks as well because it is a novel about race. He sees Clemens's work as an intersection between literary traditions of whites and African Americans. There is no question that of all of Samuel Clemens's novels, it is *Huck Finn* that confirmed him in the academy as a great American writer to be read, reread, and studied. Most likely, Mark Twain would not be read as widely in schools today (whether or not students read it or something else he wrote) if he had not written this novel.

Why is *Huck Finn* still regarded so highly today by so many writers, teachers, and educated readers? One of the reasons is that Clemens chose to tell the story from a boy's point of view in first person, in that character's own words. Giving voice to a child to narrate an entire novel was something new but also using his voice as one would hear it in-person, in other words using the *vernacular*, was an especially groundbreaking feature in literature. One question becomes evident, where did Clemens hear Huck's voice? Is it the voice of Tom Blankenship, the town drunk's son Clemens knew in Hannibal and after whom he claims in his autobiography to have patterned Huck's character?

In her book, *Was Huck Black? Mark Twain and African American Voices*, Shelley Fisher Fishkin argues, "Compelling evidence indicates that the model for Huck Finn's voice was a black child instead of a white one and that this child's speech sparked in Twain a sense of the possibilities of a vernacular narrator."[10] Fishkin claims that the novel makes more use of Clemens's early and warm acquaintance with black speech, storytelling, and culture than any of his other works. She traces Huck's voice back to an article Clemens wrote for the *New York Times* called "Sociable Jimmy," in which he first employs the voice of a child in print (Clemens also liked to record his young daughters' expressions in a private journal he kept for that purpose).

The article describes a boy Clemens met in 1871 or 1872 in a small town in the Midwest. The boy was sent to wait on him while he was dining in his room, and according to the author the boy talked and talked, not saying really anything of particular significance but talking without stopping just the same. Clemens was fascinated by the manner of Jimmy's speech and the way he let loose with it with no inhibitions whatsoever. Later he wrote to Livy about the encounter because he "wished to preserve the memory of the *most artless, sociable, and exhaustless talker I ever came across*."[11] Jimmy's language "flowed so naturally and comfortably from his lips" that Clemens became entirely engaged in the small details the boy was relating in spite of himself. Sam wrote Livy, "*I listened as one who receives a revelation*. I took down what he had to say, just as he said it—without altering a word or adding one."[12] Clemens's letter to Livy may indicate two important factors about this encounter: the revelation may have been the moment that Clemens recognized that the vernacular was as fascinating, if not more, than what was being said and that it might be possible to transfer vernacular to the page. Secondly, that the voice that drew him in with this kind of magnetism and offered this revelation came from an African American boy.

Fishkin's argument is intriguing and full of implications about the role of African American speech, stories, songs, and culture in American literature, even in places where readers may not at first look for it or notice it. Research of this sort shows how rich the novel is as a subject for serious scholarship.

If the novel is primarily about America's birth defect of the institution of slavery, the physicality of the novel itself was not without a few complications of its own in its birth process. Clemens began it the summer of 1876 at Quarry Farm, got to about chapter 16, then set it aside for three years. His next step was to work it through to about chapter 21, when he stopped again. Later, he removed an episode now commonly called "the raft chapter," and placed it within *Life on the Mississippi* and made other changes to chapters 12–14. After several more fits and starts, Clemens called the novel complete in the summer of 1883.

When the novel was typeset, there were several errors, but Clemens did not have time to make changes to the proofs. One example is that Becky Thatcher was mistakenly called "Bessie." Mistakes like these got through in the initial printing. For the 100-year anniversary of the novel's publication, scholars at the Mark Twain Papers Project at Berkeley carefully reconstructed the novel from Clemens's original manuscript and other sources, which indicated the changes he may have wanted made. Unfortunately, at that time scholars only had the latter 60 percent of the original manuscript to work with; the other portion had never been found and was believed to have been long ago lost.

Stunningly, in February 1991, the long-missing pages of the original manuscript of *Huckleberry Finn* were found. These were the first 40 percent of the book, including the first page of chapter 1. It is believed that when Clemens donated the manuscript to the Buffalo library that the same civic leader who convinced Clemens to donate the manuscript took the first part of it home to read and forgot to bring it back. It turned up in a trunk of other papers over 100 years later. Scholars have now worked to restore the novel, taking into account Clemens's markings on these long-lost original pages written in his own hand.

FAMILY AND FRIENDSHIPS

The golden years of Clemens's life not only included a good life in a grand house in Hartford, Connecticut, with peaceful summers at Quarry Farm and plenty of work, but they also marked the happiest years of the author's personal life as well. After their rough start in Buffalo during the first tragic year of their marriage, Sam and Livy had three daughters: Olivia Susan (Susy) Clemens, born March 19, 1872; Clara Langdon Clemens, born June 8, 1874; and Jane (Jean) Lampton Clemens, born July 26, 1880. Friendships Sam had established out West and in Connecticut and elsewhere provided him with the companionship he needed among people of letters as well. His marriage to Livy was, by all accounts, a happy and fulfilling one for both.

Oddly, over the years, perhaps appropriating too much of the "Aunt Polly syndrome" of the henpecked boy in *Tom Sawyer* to the real women of Clemens's life, biographers have sometimes portrayed a negative view of Livy's and other women's influence on Sam and his writing. Some have argued that Livy "tamed" him too much, that she curbed the wild imagination he was born with too tightly and reined in and watered down his work in their evening ritual of her daily edits. More recent scholars have taken a longer and more detailed view of Livy's influence and that of other women Sam knew and argue that Sam wrote more than ever with Livy in his life, that she inspired him to dig deeper and work harder rather than the other way around. Certainly Livy's sister's gift of the octagonal study at Quarry Farm can be regarded as another instance of a woman aiding and encouraging his work, and Susan Crane would doubtless never have had the study constructed if she had not seen how much the gift would also mean to her sister. It is likely the two sisters conspired to make the study available to Clemens during summers at the farm.

In all, Clemens wrote letters to over a hundred female correspondents. He helped move his sister, Pamela, and his niece to Fredonia, New York; he wrote letters to his dear mother, Jane, whom he also moved to Fredonia and who first taught him the value of storytelling. He regularly told stories by the fire to his three daughters, and his library was full of books by female authors. As Laura E. Skandera-Trombley writes in *Mark Twain in the Company of Women,* though it was true that Clemens was a "man's man," he enjoyed the company of women and respected their opinions. She writes, "In both the personal and literary realms, he was a man voluntarily controlled and influenced by women."[13]

Skandera-Trombley argues that rather than hem him in, Livy helped Clemens set limits. In a sometimes maternal role (her favorite nickname for Sam was "Youth"), Livy provided a sounding board for questions of ethics and behavior, good writing, good books, family values, and other personal and professional concerns. Theirs was an intensely close marriage, and Livy's opinion on matters of all kinds meant a great deal to Clemens. She was a cultured and refined woman brought up in the East in a secure, intact, and affectionate home. She was more formally educated than Sam was himself. Sam came from a poor, single-parent family (through no fault of his mother's after his father's early death), where affection was not something he witnessed often but which he obviously craved deeply. Livy became not only the love of his life but his moral compass and guide.

From his mother, he had inherited a love of pageantry and a lively spirit as well as the capacity to hold grudges against those he believed had wronged him. From his daughters, Sam gained ready access to his memories of childhood that became so important to the writing process of books like *Tom Sawyer, Huckleberry Finn,* and other novels. Evenings at Quarry Farm, the girls responded to passages of *Huck Finn* their father read them aloud, and Sam took their reactions into consideration as he worked on the manuscript. Though they were quite young at the time (when the novel was published, Susy was 12; Clara was 10; and Jean was four), Sam clearly valued the fresh honesty of their young opinions and their direct insights as children.

It is apparent that Clemens worked best when within earshot of his loving family but with privacy and peace during the day in which to concentrate. Since he wrote most of his fiction in this environment, the support his female family provided his emotional life seemed to release his creativity. Skandera-Trombley calls this cozy working environment Clemens's "charmed circle."[14] The degree to which Clemens's work changed, especially in a direction away from novels, when the "circle" was broken in later years adds credence to her argument. She also argues that the women among his family and friends changed his attitudes toward suffrage and other women's issues, and that his attitudes about women evolved over his lifetime to a more enlightened stance. That argument is perhaps a bit more challenging to prove, however, given the stereotypes he employs in the characterization of so many of the females in his fiction.

"PAPA"

At the age of 13, Susy Clemens began writing a biography of her father that gives an intimate portrait of this circle of love and security from which the man lived and prospered. It was later published as *Papa: An Intimate Portrait of Mark Twain by His Thirteen-Year-Old Daughter Susy, with a forword and commentary by her father*. Clemens inserts his commentary between sections of Susy's writing, which was printed intact as she wrote it, spelling, punctuation, and all. Clemens is clearly charmed by his daughter's recollections and takes her observations seriously. The result is almost a dialogue of sorts, a conversation between father and daughter recalling similar events with similar and different details, and the reader is allowed an intimate portrait of the father, the man, as well as his little girl.

"[Papa] is the loveliest man I ever saw, or ever hope to see, and oh *so* absent minded!" Susy declares. "He is a very good man, and a very funny one; he has got a temper but we all of us do in this family.... He does tell perfectly delightful stories."[15]

She tells about how Clemens "has the mind of an author exactly, some of the simplest things he can't understand."[16] By this statement she explains that her famous father has no flair for the practical whatsoever, such as fixing broken burglar alarms around the Hartford house that go off when they are not supposed to. She informs the reader that billiards is his favorite game, that when he is tired he stays up playing it all night and "it seems to rest his head."[17] He smokes too much and yells at her mother when he can't figure something out like the broken burglar alarm, which is frequently.

To this information, the author adds the comment, "This is a frank biographer and an honest one; she uses no sandpaper on me."[18] He is pained, however, when Susy speaks of his using "strong language," something he earnestly tried to curtail and keep out of the house after marrying Livy. Susy seems to know that he used it more frequently before he was married. She tells the reader that her father likes to pace when he is thinking and between courses of a meal, that he likes cats and named theirs the following names that Susy finds very funny: Stray Kit, Abner, Motly, Freulein, Lazy, Buffalo Bill, Soapy Sal, Cleveland, Sour Mash, and Famine. Many of the cats are at Quarry Farm and stroll back and forth from the study to the main house. Clearly, the man loved making his daughters giggle with his powers of language. What pleasant family evenings they must have had when the girls were young and adoring their father!

Susy consults with her father about a writer's problems in her biography, too. She says, for example, she wants to put in information about the many love letters her father wrote to her mother when they were courting, but complains that her mother has told her she is still too young to read them. The young biographer seeks her editor's advice about how to work around this problem, and the mentor tells her that writing what Mama *thinks* of the letters will do just fine.

Importantly, even at age 13, Susy is attuned to, and bothered by, the "Mark Twain" persona her father must live with in public, "... it trobles me to have so few people know papa, I mean realy know him, they think of Mark Twain as a humorist joking at every thing; and with a mop of reddish brown hair, which sorely needs the barbar's brush, a roman nose, short stubby mustache, a sad care-worn face, with many crow's feet."[19] She describes the *real* Papa this way, "... he is a very striking character... he has beautiful curly grey hair, not any too thick, or any too long, just right; A roman nose which greatly improves the beauty of his features, kind blue eyes, and a small mustache, he has a wonderfully shaped head and profile, he has a very good figure."[20] She goes on to admit, however, that his teeth, well, they are not that "extraordinary."

Susy's biography moves outward from the family setting to concern matters she witnessed in public, such as her father making speeches and meeting General Grant. Later, Clemens incorporated much of her biography in his own autobiography. He believed the child was gifted, that she held promise as a writer. It is important to note that not only was he flattered by his daughter's adoration but he also appreciated her frankness in her portrait of him and the care and detail with which she wrote. Her honesty of observation impressed him as much as the obvious love her project showed that she had for him. Small wonder if he had to pick a favorite child of the three, most observers think it would have been she.

In addition to the circle of support Clemens enjoyed from his wife and three daughters, he also benefited from friendships, both male and female, over the years. Mary Mason Fairbanks, the fellow writer he met aboard the *Quaker City*, remained a steady friend and correspondent over many years. Joseph Twichell, whom Clemens met in Hartford in 1868, was pastor of Asylum Hill Congregational Church, and seemingly an unlikely friend. He lived across the street from Clemens's Hartford publisher, Elisha Bliss, and Bliss introduced them. Twichell invited Clemens to his home on future visits, and the two respected their differing views and discussions of religion. Twichell became a good friend and counselor and took part in several significant events in Sam's life, including co-officiating at his wedding to Livy Langdon.

Clemens's ability to hold a grudge made some of his friendships, especially with other writers and business associates, sometimes tumultuous. Many of these friendships had bad endings where Clemens was hurt by some kind of misunderstanding, and never repaired ties. His friendship with writer Bret Harte is a good example. Harte befriended Clemens in San Francisco when he moved there in the mid-1860s. He had a similar upbringing to Clemens with a father who had died when he was a boy and had experience setting type in the printing industry. Harte helped Clemens with his writing career. At one time, Clemens said that it was Harte who helped transform him into a real writer in the early days. He helped Clemens edit *Innocents Abroad*, and he visited him in Hartford, and they collaborated on writing and producing a drama called *Ah Sin*, based on one of Clemens's short stories. Sometime during his visit to Hartford in 1876 and as part of the collaboration, Harte apparently did or said something that angered Clemens greatly. What the offense actually was has never been clear. He was added to Clemens's blacklist, and from then on Clemens rarely had much good to say about him, though he did still admit that Harte was a skilled writer, and he seemed to follow his career and know about his whereabouts. He detested Harte's actions of leaving his family behind to go to Europe, for example, and accused him of trying to write like Charles Dickens. With the similarities of the two men so strong in so many ways, the relationship and its downturn have intrigued scholars for years.

William Dean Howells was another well-known author and friend of Sam Clemens. Howells was a prolific writer, publishing more than a hundred books of poetry, travel, fiction, drama, sketches, criticism, essays, and biography. He and Clemens had similar backgrounds; he was from the Midwest and worked in the printing trade early in his career. He was also an editor at the *Atlantic Monthly*, and it was in this capacity in 1869 that he wrote a favorable review of Clemens's *Innocents Abroad* that Clemens appreciated and never forgot. He was so pleased with the review, in fact, that he went to the *Atlantic* office to thank Howells in person, and that is how the two met. Howells read Sam's manuscripts and offered feedback; he drew Clemens into the world of literature by publishing his work in the *Atlantic*; and he continued to give Clemens's work serious attention by reviewing his books.

Howells was a bona fide, but astute, fan of Mark Twain. Later in his career he turned to writing novels himself, but even those he regarded as his best such as *The Rise of Silas Lapham* (1885), *Indian Summer* (1886), and A

Hazard of New Fortunes (1890) did not reach the level of success or notoriety that Clemens's had. Howells regarded Clemens as unique, distinctly different in quality and kind from the New England literati who held such a stronghold on American literature in the nineteenth century. He said that Sam offered a uniquely American brand of humor and that readers responded to the overall common sense of his work. After Clemens died, Howells wrote a memoir of his times with him called *My Mark Twain*. After naming several fine writers he has known in person and whose work he values, he concludes, "Clemens was sole, incomparable, the Lincoln of our literature."[21]

DOMESTIC WORKERS AND OTHERS

Among the people in Clemens's life who have gotten more attention in recent years are the various domestic workers who cooked, cleaned, and otherwise cared for the Clemens, Crane, and Langdon families. Four of these people in particular—Katy Leary, Mary Ann Cord, George Griffin, and John Lewis—have been shown to have played an active and significant role in Sam's writing.

Katy Leary's sister, Mary, was the live-in maid of Charley Langdon's household. When the Clemenses visited Elmira in 1880, they met and hired Katy to be their maid, seamstress, and nanny to the girls, and she returned to Hartford with them. Katy ended up working for the Clemens family for 30 years. She went with them on travels and lived through, and supported them, in their tragedies. One favorite anecdote about living in the same household as Mark Twain that she liked to tell was how he would fuss at her for dusting around his manuscripts. She claimed she had not touched them, but each day Sam couldn't find certain papers he was looking for, riled himself into a tantrum over it, and blamed the mischief on Katy. Once he drew a line around his work space and disallowed her to cross it in her cleaning efforts.

As the daughter of Irish immigrants, Katy understood well how to contend with a person of occasional bad temper in the house, and she knew better than to take to heart a stretch of the truth now and then aimed in her direction. Clemens references Katy Leary in *What Is Man?* when "Young Man" speaks about an old servant of 22 years' service. Katy later dictated her memoir of working for Mark Twain to Mary Lawton and it was published in a book called *A Lifetime with Mark Twain: The Memories of Katy Leary, for Thirty Years His Faithful and Devoted Servant*. Though she was a friend of Clemens's daughter Clara, Lawton's unskillful editing made Katy sound less intelligent and articulate than she actually was. In tribute to her service, after Clemens's death, Clara gave Katy her choice of books from his personal library to take with her as the household broke up. Katy chose wisely, and her collection was kept in her family until 1994 when her great-niece, Katherine Leary Antenne and her husband Robert, gave the books to the Mark Twain Archive at Elmira College. The Antenne Collection contains several treasures, including *The Collected Verse of Rudyard Kipling* and books with Clemens's original handwritten notes in the margins.

In a 1903 young-adult novel, *Pearl Island,* by Andrew Caster from the collection, for example, there are notes in Clemens's hand that say, "The conversations in this book are incomparably idiotic." Next to one line in the novel that reads, "I saw a sailor killed at 30 feet," Clemens wrote, "I've seen it done at 29." He asks the question, "What kind of dog was it?" on one page, then sums up the novel on another as an "unhappy dog cast away with idiots on an island."

Mary Ann Cord was another employee of the family who played a part in Clemens's work even, one might go so far as to say, "co-authoring" a story called "A True Story" that was later published in the *Atlantic Monthly* in 1874. Cord was the Quarry Farm cook employed by Susan and Theodore Crane, and a former slave. Her pleasant disposition and regular peals of laughter from the family's teasing evenings on the porch after dinner caused a curious Sam Clemens one time to question how she'd managed to live 60 years without having any troubles. Mary stopped, looked at him, and proceeded to tell him a story so full of tragedy and ill fortune that Clemens wrote it down, word for word.

As a slave, Mary had lost her entire family, her husband and each of her seven children who were sold away from her one by one. After the Civil War, she was reunited with her younger son, Henry, who had escaped to the North. The story, called "A True Story Repeated Word for Word as I Heard It," underwent a bit more careful editing in manuscript than the title suggests, but the story is still Mary's true story and is now credited with contributing to Clemens's heightened awareness, sympathies, and sensibilities about slavery and the problems of African Americans. This increased awareness fed directly into the emotions of the author who wrote the classic of American literature, *Adventures of Huckleberry Finn,* which he started working on in his octagonal study at Quarry Farm two years later.

Two other domestic employees of the Clemens and Crane families may have contributed to the figure of Jim in that novel. One was George Griffin, another former slave, who worked for the Clemenses at their house in Hartford. The story goes that George walked up to the door of the Hartford house one day and asked whether they needed any windows washed.

He was hired for that work but was then also kept on the staff as Samuel Clemens's personal butler. Clemens appreciated Griffin and respected him. Griffin went to Europe with the family but his wages were probably one of the expenses the Clemenses cut when they made another trip to Europe in 1891. In 1893, Clemens ran into Griffin working in New York City and was impressed with how Griffin had fared. During bad financial times, Griffin managed to do well by working as a waiter and handling private banking for other waiters.

In Elmira, a man named John T. Lewis may have been another model for Jim. Lewis gained notoriety throughout the city when he performed a dramatic rescue of Sam's family members. He was born a free man and worked as a tenant farmer on Quarry Farm. One day in August 1877, a carriage carrying Charley Langdon's wife, Ida, daughter Julia, and a nursemaid flew down East Hill with a horse running at a wild pitch. There was a sharp turn in the road with a ravine on the other side that made for certain disaster in the minds of everyone, including Sam, who ran futilely after the carriage to try to stop it. John Lewis was coming up the hill with his horse and wagon when he saw the carriage flying toward him. Quickly, he positioned his wagon at an angle across the road that made the horse veer away from the ravine. At the same time, when the horse pulled up, John jumped from his wagon and grabbed hold of the horse's bridle in one swift motion and brought the horse and carriage to a stop.

Lewis's courage and dramatic rescue was never forgotten by the Langdon family or Sam Clemens. The farmer was rewarded in many ways, not least of which was money toward his tenant-farm arrangement and a valuable autographed copy of a novel by Mark Twain. Clemens used the rescue in a couple of his books. It was an episode that was later cut from *Pudd'nhead Wilson* but an allusion to it remains in chapter 52 of *Life on the Mississippi*.

A VISIT FROM RUDYARD KIPLING

One testament to the fame Mark Twain's name enjoyed around the world, especially at a time before television and the Internet, is the attention it garnered from Rudyard Kipling, who at the time was still unknown as a writer. Kipling came all the way to Elmira from India by way of Australia to find and meet Samuel Clemens because his writing had touched him. After several false starts, he finally arrived in Elmira in the summer of 1889 and inquired after the famous author down in the city. Someone thought the Langdons were out of town that summer; a policeman told him he thought he saw Clemens or someone who looked a lot like him driving in a buggy the day before. Finally, another person told him about Quarry Farm three miles up East Hill and that he might try there because that is where he "lives." Kipling was astonished that the townspeople treated the subject of Clemens's whereabouts so casually. Didn't they know the caliber of genius-superstar they had "living" in their midst?

Kipling hired a hack and made the climb up East Hill despite the consternation of his driver who kept complaining that no hacks drove up this steep and dusty road if they knew what was good for them. He passed the Gleason water cure and finally found the house. He described what he saw in his account of his adventure as "...a very pretty house...clothed with ivy, standing in a very big compound, and fronted by a veranda full of chairs and hammocks. The roof of the veranda was a trellis-work of creepers, and the sun peeping through moved on the shining boards below. Decidedly, this remote place was an ideal one for work, if a man could work among these soft airs and the murmur of the long-eared crops."[22]

He described a woman who came out who appeared used to redirecting callers looking for Mark Twain. She called to him that Mr. Clemens had just walked back downtown to his brother-in-law's house. Kipling had come so far to hear that he was this close that he nearly forced the driver to have an accident with how fast he demanded that they go back downhill. Finally, he was at the door of the correct house and was ushered in to meet his idol.

"Well, you think you owe me something, and you've come to tell me so," Clemens said, shaking young Kipling's hand firmly. "That's what I call squaring a debt handsomely."[23] Kipling was bowled over by Clemens's slow, calm, level voice. He was 53 years old when Kipling met him; Kipling was in his early twenties. Kipling couldn't believe that he had traveled 14,000 miles to meet this man whose books he loved, and now he had been given that opportunity and was standing in the same room smoking with the man right then and there. He barely recovered in time to realize that Clemens was talking about copyright and copyright law. He listened to him speak at length before he felt bold enough to ask some of the questions he'd come to ask.

Rudyard Kipling wanted to know if readers would ever see Tom Sawyer as a man; he wanted to know if Tom Sawyer would marry Becky Thatcher some day. Clemens answered that he had not yet decided. When he thought about it, he envisioned two futures for his character in a sequel, and he could not yet decide between them. In one version, he said, he would give Tom high honors and make him a member of Congress; in the other he would hang him. Kipling so loved Tom Sawyer and thought him real, that he protested.

Clemens agreed that indeed Tom *is* real. "He's all the boy that I have known or recollect," he said, "but that would be a good way of ending the book because, when you come to think of it, neither religion, training, nor education avails anything against the force of circumstances that drive a man. Suppose we took the next four and twenty years of Tom Sawyer's life, and gave a little joggle to the circumstances that controlled him. He would, logically and according to the joggle, turn out a rip or an angel."[24]

They talked about this philosophy for awhile. Kipling told him that Clemens couldn't give Tom Sawyer any kind of joggle and expect his audience to follow now because Tom Sawyer belonged to everyone. Clemens laughed a hearty laugh at that and went on a long diatribe about how a man owns the right to do with his creations as he will.

Next they spoke of autobiography as a form of literature. Clemens believed it was the only genre where the author could not be entirely truthful. They discussed conscience, which Clemens described as a "nuisance." They talked about novels, how Clemens read the few he did more to study their technique than to allow himself to become engaged by the story. He also talked about how he and his family lived nine months of the year in Hartford, and he counted up a typical day of interruptions there that kept him from writing. He wrote for four to five hours straight when up the hill on the farm and didn't mind an interruption here or there. "Eight or ten or twenty interruptions retard composition," he noted.[25]

Kipling had many more questions he wanted to ask. He had come so far. He wanted to know which of his works he favored and other such common questions authors get asked every day. He was captivated by Clemens's blue eyes, though, and his steady talk. Next Clemens brought up mathematics. He said that he preferred reading books of facts over fiction and advised Kipling to get his facts straight in his writing; then he was free to distort them in any way he chose. At one point in their conversation, Clemens put his hand on Kipling's shoulder, and Kipling writes that he will always as long as he lives be able to say that Mark Twain put his hand on his shoulder and shared his tobacco with him.

Once Kipling left, he thought of many more questions he should have asked and things he should have said. Clemens assured him that he had not interrupted him. Kipling went away with a lifelong memory over an encounter with an idolized writer that did not disappoint, yet sadness over what could have been said between them if they'd only had more time.

Rudyard Kipling, of course, went on to become a well-known writer in his own right. His best-known books are *The Jungle Book* (1894) and *Just So Stories* (1902), among others. Clemens did not recognize his name when his *Plain Tales from the Hills* (1888) was shown to him by his partner,

C. D. Warner, with the opinion its author would become famous. His daughter had to remind him that he was the man who'd traveled so far to Elmira just to meet him.

The two men did see each other again. Kipling moved to Vermont after his marriage to American, Caroline Balestier in 1892. Clemens saw him in April of 1893 and January of 1894. He knew Kipling's work by then and admired it. Both men were honored for their work with honorary degrees; Kipling also received the Nobel Prize for Literature. Kipling shows up in Clemens's work when he borrows several animal names from *Just So Stories* in one story, "A Fable," and in another, "Refuge of the Derelicts." Kipling's influence from the "great and godlike Clemens," as he called him, is obviously deeper than any one text can trace, but evidence is visible in his novel *Kim* (1901). The novel is about an Irish orphan who looks for the River of Immortality all throughout India accompanied by a Tibetan llama. The novel borrows themes from *Adventures of Huckleberry Finn*.

Life for Sam Clemens was fruitful and happy in the golden years of the Hartford house, summers at Quarry Farm, and times spent raising his young family. He had produced the two classics for which he is best known today as well as many other works. Family, friends, colleagues, employees, and worldwide admirers filled his days with stimulation, love and excitement, and his work was the glue that held them all together. If circumstances had not changed, just as Sam Clemens predicted to Rudyard Kipling would happen to Tom Sawyer, maybe Mark Twain would have left a different kind of legacy in his later years. As it was, circumstances were about to "joggle" Sam Clemens many times over, and it was left for time to tell whether the Tom Sawyer within him would turn out to be a rip or an angel.

NOTES

1. Qtd. in Fred Kaplan, *The Singular Mark Twain* (New York: Doubleday, 2003), p. 255..
2. Qtd. in Kaplan, *Singular*, p. 255.
3. Qtd. in Kaplan, *Singular*, p. 260.
4. Qtd. in Kaplan, *Singular*, p. 266.
5. Qtd. in Kaplan, *Singular*, p. 267.
6. Qtd. in Robert D. Jerome and Herbert A. Wisbey Jr., eds., *Mark Twain in Elmira* (Elmira N.Y.: Mark Twain Society, Inc., 1977), p. 8.
7. Qtd. in Jerome, p. 11.
8. Qtd. in J.R. LeMaster and James D. Wilson, *The Mark Twain Encyclopedia* (New York: Garland, 1993), p. 14.

9. From the original manuscript held at the Mark Twain Room, Buffalo and Erie County Public Library.

10. Shelley Fisher Fishkin, *Was Huck Black? Mark Twain and African American Voices* (New York: Oxford University Press, 1993), p. 4.

11. Qtd. in Fishkin, *Was Huck Black?*, p. 14.

12. Qtd. in Fishkin, *Was Huck Black?*, p. 15.

13. Laura E. Skandera-Trombley, *Mark Twain in the Company of Women* (Philadelphia: University of Pennsylvania Press, 1997), p. 4.

14. Skandera-Trombley, *Company*, p. 19.

15. Susy Clemens, *Papa: An Intimate Biography of Mark Twain* (Garden City, N.Y.: Doubleday, 1985), p. 84.

16. Clemens, *Papa*, p. 89.

17. Clemens, *Papa*, p. 89.

18. Clemens, *Papa*, p. 91.

19. Clemens, *Papa*, p. 106–107.

20. Clemens, *Papa*, p. 84.

21. William Dean Howells, *My Mark Twain: Reminisces and Criticisms* (New York: Harper & Brothers, 1910), p. 101.

22. Qtd. in Jerome, p. 103.

23. Qtd. in Jerome, p. 106.

24. Qtd. in Jerome, p. 106.

25. Qtd. in Jerome, p. 109.

Chapter 6

LATER YEARS: 1890–1910

The last two decades of the author's life found him fighting off tragedy and debt, illness, loneliness, and finally old age. The golden years in the house in Hartford with the summers at Quarry Farm were gone, and in their place came complex days of dealing with economic problems, personal loss, and immense grief. The latest phase of Clemens's life saddens many readers but fascinates others who find the evolution of his thoughts on such serious topics as philosophy, law, politics, religion, society, fame, and technology through these later years especially intriguing. While the subject matter of his writing became arguably more complex in theme and his books perhaps less successful or entertaining for some readers in these later years, Clemens never lost his characteristic sharp wit or attempt at good humor. The later years show readers a complicated man who had enjoyed enormous happiness and worldwide fame responding in very human and sometimes eccentric and problematic ways to a world emptying of joy for him on almost every level, one year at a time.

Though his life was undergoing significant changes, Clemens continued to write at a prolific pace. Books published from 1891 until the time of his death include: *Merry Tales* (1892); *The American Claimant* (1892); *The £1,000,000 Bank-Note and Other New Stories* (1893); *Tom Sawyer Abroad* (1894); *Tom Sawyer, Detective and Other Stories* (1896); *Personal Recollections of Joan of Arc* (1896); *How to Tell a Story and Other Essays* (1897); *Following the Equator: A Journey Around the World* (1897); *More Tramps Abroad* (1898); *The American Claimant and Other Stories and Sketches* (1899); *Literary Essays* (1899); *English As She Is Taught* (1900); *The Man That Corrupted Hadleyburg and Other Stories and Essays* (1900); A

Double-Barrelled Detective Story (1902); *My Debut as a Literary Person and Other Essays and Stories* (1903); *A Dog's Tale* (1904); *Extracts from Adam's Diary* (1904); *King Leopold's Soliloquy: A Defense of His Congo Rule* (1905); *Eve's Diary* (1906); *What Is Man?* (1906); *The $30,000 Bequest and Other Stories* (1906); *Christian Science* (1907); *A Horse's Tale* (1907); *Is Shakespeare Dead? from My Autobiography* (1909); and *Extract from Captain Stormfield's Visit to Heaven* (1909).

In addition to books, Clemens continued to publish shorter pieces in periodicals of the day as well. In fact, scholars have argued that there has yet to be compiled a complete bibliography of Mark Twain's works (if it is possible at all), since many of his works were published under other pseudonyms in the early days, and many of them appeared in obscure newspapers, magazines, or other publications. Speeches and lectures may or may not have been written down, so these are problematic for bibliographers as well. This does not even take into account the dozens of editions that have appeared after his death that gather together previously unpublished or uncollected writings.

A novel from these later years that has received more attention from scholars recently is *Pudd'nhead Wilson and Those Extraordinary Twins* (1894). The book is intriguing to early-twenty-first century critics because of its concerns with issues such as doubling and race, subjects for which Twain has become known in the study of American literature. Scholars believe that looking at *Pudd'nhead Wilson* more closely helps readers understand the whole of Clemens's work in a broader perspective, especially the subset of his extensive *oeuvre* concerned with life along the Mississippi River in the days before the Civil War.

PUDD'NHEAD WILSON

Depending on how one reads the subtitles, *Pudd'nhead Wilson* may also have the complete title of *The Tragedy of Pudd'nhead Wilson and the Comedy of Those Extraordinary Twins*. Whether Clemens wanted the words inserted between the major title lines of the original publication to actually be part of the title or simply descriptors of the title is unclear. The book does include humor, but the story is darker and concerns important issues such as slavery, miscegenation, class issues, discrimination in small towns, and family issues. The novel is constructed of 22 chapters and 53,000 words.

Clemens began writing the book as a farce about Siamese twins he saw a poster about in Europe during a trip in 1891, but as the story developed, other characters he added to it took the story in another direction. The story is set in Dawson's Landing, a small town like Hannibal, along the Mississippi River. The timeframe spans 23 years. Episodes occur in St. Louis and Arkansas, and most of the story is set in 1853. There are three major plotlines.

At the beginning of the novel, as in *The Prince and the Pauper,* two boys are born on the same day; one less fortunate than the other. In this case, a slave woman, Roxy, switches her son, Chambers, with her master's son, Tom Driscoll. The boys grow up and live the very different experiences that their respective places in society put upon them but with interesting twists and turns along the way. "Tom Driscoll," for example, the slave's son, grows up to murder his presumed uncle for money and is found out. The second storyline involves attorney David Wilson whose career is compromised after he makes a comment on arriving in Dawson's Landing. The third plot concerns Italian twins, Angelo and Luigi Capello, who arrive in Dawson's Landing in chapter 5.

Pudd'nhead Wilson was originally serialized in the *Century Magazine*. Sam Clemens read the proofs for this publication and corrected them, so of the various subsequent printings of the novel, the serialized version is considered by scholars to be the most authentic. For the book publication, Clemens removed much of the section about the Siamese twins, but scholars believe that the context of the *Wilson* novel is lost if readers do not read the *Twins* section as well, so most editions printed more recently contain both. In a novel at least in part about doubling, it is ironic that the novel itself has been "doubled" or halved. In this way, the construction of the novel somewhat mirrors one of its themes. The unevenness of its editing, in addition, suggests to those who find the novel interesting that its errors and oddities mirror ambiguities and ambivalences in society about many of the issues the novel is addressing.

Scholars are intrigued by the novel's strange organization and the disruption of a continuous plot and theme, problems that normally are required to be resolved for a novel to be successful. Clemens was writing quickly at this period to make money in order to assuage the losses he incurred from the Charles Webster Company and the Paige typesetter. He wrote more than 60,000 words between November 12 and December 14, 1891—6,000 in one 13-hour day. The novel is a study of an author getting into deeper and deeper water in terms of sophisticated themes while at the same time needing to get the work done as quickly as possible so that it could be published and start making much needed money for his family. The struggle for artistic integrity and the pull of narrative vs. commercial value makes for a fascinating dynamic and possibly stands as a metaphor for much of Clemens's life struggles in the later years of his life.

BUSINESS FAILURES

One of the character flaws Sam Clemens seems to have inherited from his father, John Clemens, was a chronic inability to make good business decisions. Clemens was interested in technology and thought that big money could be made quickly from investing in the latest gadget coming out of research and development. He poured money into product after product, even inventing some himself. Most made very little, if any, profit, but the recurrent losses did not discourage Clemens from trying again on the next great idea to come along. In some ways, his blindness about the repeated large failures suggests parallels to an obsession with gambling.

Clemens's interest in machines and new technology was genuine. He was fascinated by the machines he saw on display, for example, at the Crystal Palace World's Fair in New York City when he first went there in 1853, and seeing Benjamin Franklin's actual printing press in Philadelphia that same year caused him to marvel at how far printing methods had progressed since Franklin's day. His work as a printer and even as a steamboat pilot showed at least a familiarity with machines and their basic principles. In the Hartford house, Clemens had a central-heating gas furnace and a telephone. It was said his was the first residence to have either.

His daughter Susy's observation, however, that her father was all-thumbs when it came to practical matters such as fixing burglar alarms, that he was an author "entirely," shows how there was some aptitude for understanding machinery that Clemens must have found missing. Taking this lack of knowledge and adding to it a poor sense of timing and feel for what people wanted or were willing to buy, put him in debt time and time again from investing too heavily and losing his money. Among others, some products he invested in include a steam generator, an envelope maker, an engraver, a carpet-pattern machine, an advanced cash register, a steam pulley, a special telescope, and plasmon (a food additive). Products he invented included a self-pasting scrapbook (which did make some money), a history game, a spiral hairpin, a calendar watch fob, and a self-adjusting vest strap.

As one who kept newspaper clippings and other papers in a scrapbook himself, Clemens grew annoyed with working with glue each time he wanted to stick something in one of the books. He invented pages that had glue already on them that users could moisten when they wanted to stick something to the page. The idea was patented and, Dan Slote, a Clemens friend, produced the scrapbooks in different sizes and with specialized pages for photographs and various clippings, and offered them for sale. In 1877, Clemens sold about 25,000 of them with a profit of around $12,000. Sales dwindled quickly, but the product stands as the only good investment of this kind that Clemens made.

Clemens invested about $50,000 in something called the Kaolatype. This was a new method of printing illustrations in books and magazines. This project failed because it came about at the same time as other more superior methods were also being developed.

By far the most costly loss Clemens incurred was his $300,000 investment in the largest machine yet called the Paige Compositor. As a former printer, it seems that Clemens would have had an acute eye for the machine that would revolutionize the movable-type printing industry, but such was not the case. The Paige was supposed to replace the human typesetter, serving as a kind of robot for the actions a human being normally performed. The Paige typesetter failed to catch on, trial after trial and adjustment after adjustment. Clemens believed in the product too long and tried too hard to make a go of it when he should have long before abandoned it and cut his losses. He invested not only too much of his book profits in the machine, but alarmingly too much of Livy's inheritance as well. It was the Paige typesetter chiefly, combined with other poor investments that caused the ruin of his family financially. From 1885 through 1894 alone, Clemens invested $3,000 to $4,000 a month in unprofitable machines.

Not only did investments in machines turn out to be poor business decisions for Clemens but also his efforts at forming a publishing company; the Charles L. Webster Company, named after Clemens's partner in the business, ran into financial troubles. Webster had a promising start. After all, its inaugural publication was the first American edition of *Adventures of Huckleberry Finn*! The firm also won the contract to publish Ulysses S. Grant's memoir. Perhaps hoping to keep up with the success of these first two giants was part of the company's downfall. Webster & Company published memoirs of other Civil War generals such as Crawford, Hancock, McClellan, Sheridan, and Sherman. Other authors it published included stars such as Leo Tolstoy and Walt Whitman. Of all of these, however, it was Mark Twain's books that sold the most and made the most profit for the company.

Almost predictably, it was a series of Clemens's poor decisions and the Clemens family curse of bad business luck that drove the company into bankruptcy. One was to offer a $5,000 advance to Henry Ward Beecher for his autobiography—he died two months later. Another was the commissioning of an authorized biography of Pope Leo XIII. Nobody bought it. Still another was hiring a bookkeeper who later embezzled $25,000 from the company. An 11-volume anthology of American literature called the *Library of American Literature* was a good idea that sold well, but profits were slow coming in on the subscription plan under which buyers paid for it. Added to all of these problems was Clemens's "addiction" to the Paige Compositor—he took money from the Webster publishing company to more deeply invest in the Paige. On April 18, 1894, the Webster Company declared bankruptcy, and Clemens had to do something to get a great deal of money quickly.

In June, 1891, the financial strain of the failed Paige typesetter, and the growing losses of the Webster Company, and the lavish lifestyle at the Hartford mansion created such economic hardship on the family that the only way Sam and Livy knew to support themselves was to close up the house in Hartford and move to Europe, where they could live reasonably close to the lives they were used to but at a fraction of the cost. They loved the house and the memories it held for them as a family so dearly that they did not sell it right away but held out hope that some day they might be able to afford to return.

As expatriates, the Clemenses moved from rental house to summer villa to apartment throughout Europe, seemingly never content in any one place for long. Their trips back and forth to the States over the next few years, where they also lived in temporary housing in such places as Maine, spread their restless lifestyle across two continents. By losing the Hartford house in 1891 and going so far into debt, the family lost its anchor. By losing the Webster Company in 1894, they nearly lost their shirts.

If Sam made mistakes, and big ones, however, he was a man who faced up to his responsibility to make things right. He determined that a world lecture tour would earn enough money to pay back every penny, even though legally he was only liable for about half of his original debt. The tour was arranged, and the 60-year-old Clemens planned to pay back his faults and bring back his family from financial ruin using the old skill that stood by him when he'd needed it years ago when he was a single man—as the now world-famous Mark Twain, he'd go out on the lecture circuit once again and tell stories to people who would pay to listen.

SUSY'S DEATH

When the family returned to the States after four years in Europe, Susy Clemens didn't want to travel again on the long world tour of 1895. She had dropped out of Bryn Mawr to go to Europe in 1891 (there may have been more complicated reasons for her leaving college as well), and she'd put her dreams of writing and singing on hold. She and Jean both wanted to stay in Elmira with their Aunt Susan Crane, so the two sisters did so while Clara accompanied their parents on the trip. The plan was that at the conclusion of the lecture tour, the family would all meet up again in London.

As the Clemenses made it back to England, Susy was visiting Hartford to prepare for the voyage to London to meet her parents when she asked Katy Leary to delay their departure because she felt ill. At first Katy did not think it was serious, but when Susy's fever heightened, she called a doctor, who diagnosed spinal meningitis. Meanwhile, on the other side of the Atlantic, Sam and Livy were getting mixed signals. First, there was a telegram telling them there had been a delay in the girls' departure, then another that Susy was ill. There were several hours of no news at all, and Livy became worried enough that she booked tickets for herself and Clara on the next boat out of Southampton. She told Sam that he should stay in England to take care of any family issues that might need to be addressed there. When they finally received another telegram, it simply stated that Susy's recovery would take a long time, but that it was certain she would get better. Livy and Clara were on their way.

Sam felt dreadful as he waved to Livy until she and Clara were out of sight as the ship headed for the open ocean on Saturday, August 15, 1896. He felt he'd brought all of this on the family through his reckless business dealings. If he had only not made such poor investments the family could have stayed together in the Hartford house. Susy was there now without them. He feared for the worst.

Another telegram finally arrived on Tuesday, August 19, and was the saddest one he'd ever received. It read, "Susy could not stand brain congestion and meningitis and was peacefully released to-day."[1] Susy had died in the Hartford house on the evening of the 18th, Hartford time. Livy and Clara were still two days away from New York. The captain of the ship asked to speak with Clara the next day. When she went up to him, he handed her a dispatch that read, "Mark Twain's Eldest Daughter Dies of Spinal Meningitis." Clara went back to their cabin. As soon as Livy saw her, she knew and burst into tears, crying out that she couldn't believe it. The woman who, as a young girl had so idolized her father that she wrote a biography of him, was gone.

When they reached New York, several friends met them at the dock. They went to Elmira, where Livy found her daughter's coffin laid out in the same Langdon parlor where she and Susy's father had married. It was decided that Sam would stay in England because it would delay the burial too long to wait for him to sail across, so Livy had to go through the ordeal of the funeral and burial at Woodlawn Cemetery without him. Still, Sam envied her chance to look at Susy one more time, an opportunity he would not have. He knew subconsciously even then that the only way he could hope to keep his sanity through this dreadful tragedy was to throw himself into his work. Clara said later he never worked more rigorously in his life than the months following Susy's death. Perhaps he also thought through more and better work, he might find redemption for his sins against the family.

Livy felt her family's hearts were broken and would never heal again, and she was right. She and Clara did go back to England to live with Sam, but life would never be the same again. Livy sat day after day staring at nothing and tried to figure out what had happened. She read from Susy's copy of Tennyson's *In Memorium*, which offered only partial comfort. Long before this, she had fallen away from the church as a result of Sam's influence and disbelief.

A little over a year later, in mid-December 1897, a telegram arrived from Keokuk informing Sam that his 73-year-old brother, Orion, whom he had not seen in over 10 years, was dead.

LIVY'S DEATH

In his reference book about the holdings of the Clemens library, Alan Gribben notes that the last entry in Livy's commonplace book came from Ralph Waldo Emerson's essay, "The Over-Soul": "In sickness, in languor, give us a strain of poetry or a profound sentence, and we are refreshed; or produce a volume of Plato or Shakespeare or remind us of their names and instantly we come into a feeling of longevity."[2]

The Clemenses had returned to New York after the turn of the century. Sam made a visit to Hannibal in 1901, where he was photographed as a celebrity returning home. There are snapshots of him outside his boyhood home and others of him at the depot holding a gift bouquet of flowers. Hannibal was already on its way toward making its connections to Mark Twain a profitable enterprise.

He and Livy made a last visit to Elmira and Quarry Farm in 1903. They thought it might help Livy's health as it had so many times all those summers ago. The trip was another melancholy one, one that filled both of them with sadness and longing for the past. Clemens posed for a few photographs here, too—some on the veranda with Livy; one with John Lewis on the porch steps looking down at the beloved valley, some at the study now overgrown with vines, another on the stone steps leading up the hillside to the study from the house. The pose of Clemens on the steps was later adapted into a statue that now stands on the campus of Elmira College. It was a gift to the college from the class of 1934 and features Clemens standing on octagonal steps with the titles of books he wrote at Quarry Farm engraved on them.

Jean suffered from epilepsy and her bouts with seizures seemed to increase as Livy's condition worsened. She had no career, nor plans for one, since her own health was so poor and unpredictable and treatments in those days were unsatisfactory. The beloved house in Hartford that they had abandoned was not selling. Finally, Clemens accepted a grossly low offer of $25,000 just to unload it. He never wanted to see it again after Susy had died there.

They went back to Europe, this time to Florence, Italy, again for Livy's health. Clara pursued a singing career as best she could there and had a romance interrupted by the moving around and constant care of her mother. The strain was taking its toll on her young adult life, and once she got so angry that she flew into a rage and broke furniture, yelling that she hated her father and mother. Immediately afterward, she was filled with remorse.

For long intervals in his wife's treatment, Sam was not allowed to see Livy any more than five minutes at a time to help her avoid excitement. He spent his time writing letters to her and waiting for the appointed time when he could see her once again. When she seemed to feel better, he played some old spirituals on the piano. These songs he heard in his youth at the Quarleses' farm in Missouri seemed to come out of him when he was in touch with his deepest feelings. Livy's days of feeling better were short-lived, however, and Sam, Clara, and Jean all knew she was dying.

On June 6, 1904, Katy Leary was out, and Jean and Clara sat with their mother. The nurse had given her oxygen during the day. Sam visited for his time that evening, and he and Livy talked about a new rented villa they planned to move into later that summer. The nurse returned and asked Sam and Clara to leave. Katy came back around nine o'clock. Livy told Katy that she had been sick all afternoon. "You'll be all right now," Katy said, leaning over her and taking her in her arms.[3] Katy remembered later that Livy took a short breath and fell over on Katy's shoulder. Sam appeared, whether from instinct or from Katy's call, no one is sure. Clara also came in. Sam bent over his wife's relaxed face and thought he spoke to her and was concerned when she didn't seem to recognize him or respond. Clara and Jean started crying and threw their arms around their father's neck, and all three of them wept from the excruciating pain of broken hearts.

POLITICS AND RELIGION

While Sam Clemens never ran for public office and was primarily known as a humorist, his notoriety around the country and around the world made his views on such important issues as politics and religion of interest to many of those who read them. In his later years, Clemens thought more about these matters and found himself increasingly in settings where he was either asked for his opinion on various issues of the day or asked to philosophize on the great questions of religion and life's meaning much as a statesman or a sage.

Clemens denounced imperialism, the desire to spread one's own country's power and values worldwide. He was a master of the political satire, often lampooning candidates he disagreed with in print, but always with humor. Rather than focus on individuals in individual races, however, his satire tended to be directed toward ideas or movements rather than specific candidates. Newspapers and politics have always been closely associated in America, and Clemens came at the subject much as a journalist. As he became more worldly from his wide travels, he expanded his views to have concerns about the role the United States could play in the world.

Sam Clemens had an ongoing fight with God. In many long discussions with his friend Joe Twichell he tried hard to either believe or understand those who did with more compassion. One story goes that one night he knelt beside Twichell and prayed for faith. Most of the time, he argued that human beings are shaped by what he described to Rudyard Kipling as "circumstances," that there is little one could do to effect a particular outcome but respond to any given situation one finds oneself in.

Clemens dabbled some in Christian Science because he was impressed by what he heard about healings brought about by the mind. He wrote an article about the new religion, founded by Mary Baker Eddy in 1879, in which he predicts a rapid growth in its membership. By 1930, he expected there would be 20 million members and that by 1940, the church would control the religious thinking of the country.

After close study and because Eddy's writing was uneven and incomprehensible in some instances, Clemens began to question whether she actually wrote the doctrine, *Science and Health*, herself or whether she was merely a money-hungry sham. He began to write negatively about the religion by 1907, and targeted Eddy specifically.

Many readers of Clemens's later thoughts on politics and religion find a pessimistic, sometimes bitter, man who did not believe in an afterlife and who believed that the future of the United States was less than appealing in terms of its contributions to the world. Others read a social critic who never let up on telling the truth as he saw it, who loved his country enough to warn it against its own faults in the same way as he admitted his own, and who refused to compromise the rights of the individual for the gain of a powerful bureaucracy.

WHITE SUITS

If one of Livy's roles in Sam's life had been to set limits, then when she left him, all boundaries were removed. Many observers see Livy's death as the beginning of a downward turn in Clemens, both in his life and in his writing, but others see a man who was affected deeply by her loss but was not broken by it.

In his later years (Clemens would outlive Livy by six years), the author developed a few eccentricities, or rather perhaps it might be better said that his tendencies toward the eccentric knew no limits. One of the oddities he developed (as others saw it) was the frequent wearing of white suits. In personal appearances as well as at less formal occasions, Clemens showed up in all times of year wearing a summer suit of white pants, jacket, and vest. It was said he walked down the streets of New York City when people would be getting out of church just to see them look at him. Whether this is true or not is unclear.

Clemens didn't always wear white, but he wore it at enough noteworthy occasions from age 71 onward to develop a reputation for it as a trademark of his later years. For example, he wore a white suit in the dead of winter to a Congressional hearing on copyright in Washington, D.C. He made a speech about white clothing at London's Savage Club in 1907 and, fittingly, wore a white suit there. The suits may or may not have been intended as some kind of statement. Once, Clemens said that he preferred wearing white because at his age dark clothing was depressing; there was so much darkness in the world that he wanted to cheer himself and other folks up. Another reason given by scholars was simply that he had a penchant for cleanliness, and he liked looking clean. Still another was that a white suit always attracted attention, and it served as a sort of costume for the caricature of Mark Twain that Sam Clemens had created.

Today scholars say that the image of Clemens in a white suit is overplayed. Many readers mistakenly think that he wore white suits during lecture tours and that he wore them earlier than he did. In fact, Clemens's lecture-tour days were over by the time he was seen wearing them.

OXFORD HONORARY DOCTORATE

Dress in his later years does continue to be an intriguing issue, however. Clemens received what he regarded as one of the highest, if not the highest honor of his life on June 26, 1907, when he received an honorary doctorate of laws degree at Oxford University in England. The story goes that a few months before the ceremony, the editor of the *London Times*, C. F. Moberly Bell, met Clemens and asked him when he was coming back to England. Having decided against traveling abroad again, Clemens announced that the only way he would go back is if Oxford awarded him an honorary degree (this said in the spirit of "when hell freezes over"). That May, he received a cable from Lord Cruzon, the new chancellor of Oxford, who offered him the degree.

The timing of Clemens's voyage to England aboard the S. S. *Minneapolis* must have suggested to Clemens that this honor was meant to be. He sailed on June 8, 1907, exactly 40 years after he first set sail across the Atlantic on the *Quaker City*. He had sailed that voyage 40 years ago before he met Livy, so not having Livy with him for this trip must have been made a little easier by thinking back on old times.

Clemens's final trip to England was triumphant in all respects. He was lauded all over London; he was given a garden party by King Edward VII and met with the highest society of the British literary scene. At the ceremony, he received his honor alongside several other noteworthy awardees, namely, Rudyard Kipling, the writer who had sought him out in Elmira; Auguste Rodin, the artist; Camille Saint-Saëns; and General William Booth of the Salvation Army. Thomas A. Edison was to be also honored, but he refused to participate.

Clemens posed for several photographs wearing his academic regalia. The distinction meant a great deal to him as a man who grew up on the Mississippi River with so little formal education. Without Livy around to help set limits on his apparent lack of good taste, however, Clemens came back to the United States and began wearing the cap and gown at all kinds of occasions. There is even one photograph of him wearing it over a white suit at his daughter Clara's wedding.

ANGELFISH

About this same time in his early 70s, Clemens began complaining that he had no grandchildren. He missed the sound of his three young daughters, long since gone or grown, around the house and began making acquaintances with mothers and girls he met while on his travels. They struck up correspondences. Soon, he formed a club he called the "Aquarium Club," ostensibly to enjoy the company of the adolescent girls, share books, and play games. Even more strangely, Clemens told others that some people collect art or other collectibles; he collected young girls as pets. With their parents' approval, these girls wrote back and forth to Sam and went to his house for afternoon meetings of the club. He met a few girls while on a trip to Bermuda, and they went to see the sites together. Sam called these young female friends, his "Angelfish."

Over the last five years of his life, Sam Clemens wrote 300 letters to the Angelfish. The "Club" consisted of 12 "official" members: Dorothy Butes, Carlotta Welles, Frances Nunnally, Dorothy Quick, Margaret Blackmer, Irene Gerken, Dorothy Sturgis, Hellen Martin, Helen Allen, Marjorie Breckenridge, Dorothy Harvey, and Louise Paine, daughter of Clemens's authorized biographer, Albert Bigelow Paine. Gertrude Natkin was an early correspondent but was not part of the Aquarium Club.

Though no one so far seems to accuse Sam of impropriety in his dealings with these girls (he seemed to value their innocence above all), Clara for one did not approve of this odd behavior on the part of her father. For whatever reason, Clara and Jean were not as close to their father in adulthood as they had been as girls. Most likely, they were less patient with him and his ways than Livy had been, and when she was no longer there to temper him and help things run smoothly, and he no longer had her to try to live up to, the daughters' feelings got hurt from his tantrums. Perhaps grudges developed along with the Clemens pride they would have all shared, and hurdles became increasingly difficult to get over. It is ironic that the very thing Clemens was missing that caused him to adopt this odd behavior—family—was the very thing he warded off by engaging in keeping young girls around him.

STORMFIELD AND JEAN

Jean's epilepsy worsened after her mother's death. She was institutionalized. During seizure episodes in 1905 and 1906, she tried to kill Katy Leary. Depending on her condition, she was in and out of sanitariums. Living with her father did not always help. Her illness and frequent travels with her family into her early adulthood prevented her from establishing many interests or romances. Jean did love animals and did some work for animal rights. In 1908, she went to Germany with a friend seeking treatment. By April, 1909, she moved back to Stormfield in Redding, Connecticut, Samuel Clemens's last home.

In building Stormfield, (named after the book that paid for the house) Sam hoped to end the days of wandering that he and his family had been plagued by since they closed up the house in Hartford. Albert Bigelow Paine had suggested the location—248 acres on Redding Road about three and one-half miles from Redding's train station and not far from Paine's own home. Clara oversaw the construction of the 18-room Italianate villa designed by William Dean Howells's son, John Mead Howells. Sam wanted nothing to do with that aspect of things. He didn't want to move in until everything was finished and the house furnished right down to the cat purring by the hearth. When he moved in on June 18, 1908, after returning from a trip to Bermuda for his health, everyone was pleased that he liked the results. With his large new home, it seemed that Sam was beginning to realize that he needed grounding, whether Livy was alive to give it to him or not. Moving into Stormfield was probably the beginning of an upturn in his spirits. The rooms were large enough for his orchestrelle (a player-piano-like instrument), and the views of the Saugatuck Valley and streams gurgling through his land offered promise that he might at last find some peace from the last few tragic and wandering years.

The house quickly began developing a history of its own. In September, it was burglarized, with some sentimental pieces of silver stolen. The next month, Clara was married at Stormfield. Clemens spent his days there dictating his autobiography to Paine. Isabel Lyon, his personal secretary, took on many of the business matters that Livy once had been so good at handling. There were disputes between Clara and Lyon when Clemens turned over power-of-attorney of his business affairs to Lyon and Ralph Ashcroft, another business advisor. Clara became almost as difficult to deal with as Sam.

The Christmas of 1909, Sam and Jean were getting along well. Jean threw herself into decorating Stormfield for the holidays as her mother used to do in Hartford. She put up a tree, and fresh garland graced the mantle. He and Jean enjoyed a couple of quiet, pleasant evenings before Christmas. The night before Christmas Eve, they walked hand-in-hand from the dinner table to the library and stayed up late talking. Finally, when it came time to turn in, Jean told her father she'd best not kiss him because she had a cold. He bent to kiss her hand, and she was obviously moved and bent to kiss his as well. Then they each retired.

The next morning, Sam awoke hearing voices and commotion in the house. Katy Leary burst into his room and announced that Jean was dead, that she had died in her morning bath, probably of a heart attack. Sam later wrote in his autobiography, "Possibly I know now what the soldier feels when a bullet crashes through his heart."[4]

Sam spent Christmas going through Jean's things. He found her Christmas gift to him—a globe that he'd always wanted. He found a collection of his books stacked up that he knew she was probably going to ask him to sign for a gift she was planning to send away. Katy dressed her in the gown she wore for Clara's wedding.

Sam's health was too poor to make the trip with Jean to Elmira. They came to take her Christmas night. Albert Paine played the orchestrelle as they took her casket. He played Schubert's *Impromptu* for Jean, her favorite. He played *Intermezzo* for Susy, and *Largo* for their mother. These were requested by Sam as he said good-bye. The dog, whom Jean loved was said to be the first mourner in the room. He jumped up and looked at her face. Clemens said he *knew.*

Sam watched the hearse drive slowly off with Katy Leary and Jervis Langdon, Jean's cousin, in attendance. The day after Christmas at 2:30 P.M., Sam wrote in his autobiography as the funeral would be proceeding, living it with the mourners as best he could from a distance. He could see the coffin in the Langdon parlor in Elmira where he had stood to marry Livy, where Susy's coffin had laid, and Livy's had later. By 5 o'clock, he wrote that it was over.

With Clara in Europe, Livy and Susy both dead, Sam had thought he and Jean might have a chance at recreating a small piece of family life again for themselves. Jean was happy and eager to try, and they'd made plans for rebuilding a warm homelife at Stormfield the night they'd stayed up late talking. Now Jean was gone, too, and the great, grand house seemed larger and colder than ever.

LAST DAYS

During his last voyage to Bermuda for his health just months after Jean's death, Clemens asked his chosen biographer, Albert Bigelow Paine, to read *Jude the Obscure* by Thomas Hardy so that they could discuss it. This was April 9–11, 1910, and the novel is regarded as the last book Clemens read before he died. He suffered from angina, a heart ailment, and was in and out of good days and spirits. Nevertheless, he began to speak as though he was aware that the end was near.

Clara was on her way home from Europe to be with him, but at first Sam wanted to stay in Bermuda and not travel back home at all. He was feeling truly miserable and weak. Soon, however, he changed his mind and said that he did not want to die there. Sam had to make the long voyage home, and he was deteriorating rapidly. Albert Paine had injections of morphine from the doctor with him and was allowed to administer it to keep Clemens comfortable. Once Clemens asked that he give him enough to end it all, but Paine asked him to hang on until they could get back to New York for Clara's sake. Clemens ordered that when the time came he did not want to be resuscitated.

Clemens survived his last journey by boat. Fans, journalists, and well-wishers watched as perhaps the most famous man in the world was taken off the ship in New York Harbor. Just as he was lifted to the dock, he felt the familiar pain in his chest again and became chilled in the New York spring air. He boarded the train to Redding, got off and walked into Stormfield on his own, then went to bed. Two days later Clara and Ossip arrived. It is unknown whether she told her father on his deathbed that she was then four months pregnant, but Katy Leary, who was at his bedside continually as she had been for so many of the Clemens family, probably knew.

Clemens was sedated with morphine much of the time to stay comfortable, and he was in and out of consciousness. He rarely spoke and when he did it was either incoherent or unintelligible.

He wrote Clara a note on April 21. The note read, "Dear You did not tell me, but I have found out that you..." [5] The note may have been an attempt to let her know that he knew after all that she was expecting, but there is no way to know for sure. Late in the evening he scrawled another note in a ragged, nearly unintelligible hand, "bring me my spectacles / bring me my glass / pitcher."[6] They were the last words that Samuel Clemens ever wrote.

He died peacefully at sunset on April 21, 1910. Later that year Halley's Comet would streak across the sky as it had during the year he was born. On Shakespeare's birthday, April 23, thousands of people streamed past the author's open casket in Brick Presbyterian Church, Manhattan. His old friend Joe Twichell said a public prayer. The nation hung black mourning cloths on public buildings as they do when a president dies. At a memorial service William Dean Howells said, "I wish we might show him frankly as he always showed himself."[7] President William Taft, who had closely followed news of Clemens's deteriorating health which was broadcast around the world, put out a press release:

> Mark Twain gave pleasure—real intellectual enjoyment—to millions, and his works will continue to give such pleasure to millions yet to come. He never wrote a line that a father could not read to a daughter. His humor was American, but he was nearly as much appreciated by Englishmen and people of other

countries as by his own countrymen. He has made an enduring part of American literature.[8]

Samuel Clemens, the man who missed his family so dearly in the later year of his life, was buried next to Livy, Langdon, Susy, and Jean in Woodlawn Cemetery, Elmira, New York. A monument two fathoms high, "mark twain," marks the grave. Over Susy's grave years before, Clemens had the following words engraved, which he adapted from the final lines of the poem "Annette" in the collection *Willow and Wattle* (1893) by Robert Richardson:

Warm summer sun, shine kindly here;
Warm southern winds, blow softly here;
Green sod above, lie light, lie light;
Good night, dear heart, good night, good night.[9]

LEGACY

Samuel Clemens is a permanent fixture of American literature. It is nearly impossible for any serious student or scholar of the discipline to get very far without encountering, and having to come to terms with, in one way or another, the work and personage of Mark Twain. Whether one reads his work as a beacon that sheds insights on the nation's literature that came before it as well as after it or as merely a bump in the road that has received more attention than it's worth, Mark Twain is an American writer who must be dealt with. Ernest Hemingway's twentieth-century claim that *Huckleberry Finn* is "the best book we've had. All American writing comes from that" perhaps kept this dynamic running within the academy, but Sam Clemens himself set it in motion over 100 years ago, partly by writing books that so many readers enjoyed and partly by being America's most popular export. Even today, if you ask young readers from other countries to name an American author, Mark Twain is quite often the first (and many times only) name that comes to their lips.

Before Sam Clemens began writing his best novels, much American fiction was still written in a language close to a more formal British English. In many ways, Clemens is to American fiction what Whitman is to its poetry. He opened up a new way of telling stories that could only be told by Americans who grew up on this continent, breathed the air, swam in its rivers, and dug for treasures of gold and silver as though it were their birthright to do so. In particular, he translated the sounds of speech in this country to the written word.

Whether the ending works or not, whether the pacing of the novel is uneven or there are chapters that could have been left out, the moment Huck tears up the note to Miss Watson and says if freeing Jim will damn himself, then he'll "go to hell," something clicked in the American collective psyche that set it on a new path toward self-examination and knowledge. There was an opportunity to look at racism head-on, to self-examine, and perhaps redeem past mistakes. If young Huck could change through finding out that one person seemingly different from himself actually wasn't so different, well, then, perhaps others could do that as well.

Sam Clemens would be the first man in the room to say that he was not a perfect man and that he was not a perfect writer. He appreciated Susy not "sandpapering" him in the biography she wrote of him as a young girl. Perhaps Huck himself sums up Clemens's legacy best when he says, "Mr. Mark Twain . . . he told the truth, mainly. There was things he stretched, but mainly he told the truth."

NOTES

1. Qtd. in Fred Kaplan, *The Singular Mark Twain* (New York: Doubleday, 2003), p. 534.
2. Qtd. in Alan Gribben, *Mark Twain's Library: A Reconstruction*, 2 vols. (Boston: G.K. Hall & Co., 1980) p. 221.
3. Qtd. in Kaplan, *Singular*, p. 611.
4. Neider, *Autobiography*, p. 486.
5. Qtd. in Kaplan, *Singular*, p. 654.
6. From photo of note in Milton Meltzer, *Mark Twain Himself: A Pictorial Biography* (St. Louis: University of Missouri Press, 2002), p. 287.
7. Qtd. in Kaplan, *Singular*, p. 654.
8. http://etext.lib.virginia.edu/railton/sc_as_mt/obitap.html
9. Qtd. in "The Poem on Susy Clemens's Headstone," http://www.twainquotes.com/headstone.html (accessed 27 April 2004).

Appendix A

CLEMENS FAMILY TREE

FIRST GENERATION

James Marshall Clemens (b. August 11, 1798; d. March 24, 1847)	Father
Jane Lampton (b. June 18, 1803; d. October 27, 1890)	Mother

SECOND GENERATION

Orion Clemens (b. July 17, 1825; d. December 11, 1897)	Brother
Pamela Ann Clemens (b. September 13, 1827; d. August 31, 1904)	Sister
Pleasant Hannibal Clemens (b. 1828 or 1829; d. aged 3 months)	Sister
Margaret L. Clemens (b. May 31, 1830; d. August 17, 1839)	Sister
Benjamin L. Clemens (b. June 8, 1832; d. May 12, 1842)	Brother
SAMUEL LANGHORNE CLEMENS (b. November 30, 1835; d. April 21, 1910)	**The Author**
Henry Clemens (b. July 13, 1838; d. June 21, 1858)	Brother

MARRIAGES:

Orion m. Mary Eleanor (Mollie) Stotts (1834–1904) on Dec. 19, 1854

Pamela m. William Anderson Moffett (1816–1865)
on Sept. 20, 1851

Samuel m. Olivia Louise (Livy) Langdon (1845–1904)
on Feb. 2, 1870

THIRD GENERATION

Orion and Mollie's children:

Jennie Clemens (b. Sept. 14, 1855; d. Feb. 1, 1864) — Niece

Pamela and William's children:

Annie E. Moffett (b. July 1, 1852; d. Mar. 24, 1950)

m. Charles Luther Webster (1851–1891) — Niece

Samuel Erasmus Moffett (b. Nov. 5, 1860; d. Aug. 1, 1908)
m. Mary Emily Mantz (1863–1940) — Nephew

Samuel and Livy's children:

Langdon Clemens (b. Nov. 7, 1870; d. June 2, 1872) — Son

**Olivia Susan (Susy) Clemens (b. Mar. 19, 1872;
d. Aug. 18, 1896) — Daughter**

**Clara Langdon Clemens (b. June 8, 1874;
d. Nov. 19, 1962) — Daughter**
m. Ossip Gabrilowitsch (1878–1936)
m. Jacques Alexander Samoussoud (1894–1966)

**Jane Lampton (Jean) Clemens (b. July 26, 1880;
d. Dec. 24, 1909) — Daughter**

FOURTH GENERATION

Annie and Samuel Webster's children:

Alice Jane (Jean) Webster (1876–1916) — Grandniece and author*

William Luther Webster (1878–1945) — Grandnephew

Samuel Charles Webster (1884–1962) — Grandnephew

*Jean Webster, Samuel Clemens's grandniece, wrote the 1912 novel *Daddy-Long-Legs* as well as other works.

SAMUEL AND MARY MOFFETT'S CHILDREN:

Anita Moffett (1891–1952)	Grandniece
Francis Clemens Moffett (1895–1927)	Grandnephew
Clara and Ossip Gabrilowitsch's children:	
Nina Gabrilowitsch (b. Aug. 18, 1910; d. Jan. 16, 1966)	Granddaughter

Appendix B

SAMUEL CLEMENS'S READING

The selected list of works below are mentioned either by Samuel Clemens himself, those who knew him, or have been found through evidence in his letters, notebooks, journals, books, or other documents to be titles read by the author. In cases where the listing comes from a book found in the Clemens (Hartford) or Langdon/Crane (Elmira) libraries, marginalia or comments elsewhere were used as evidence for whether the author actually read the work.

In addition to using his well-known firsthand experience as the subject matter for his work, Joe B. Fulton argues that Clemens also researched books for his novels more than has been previously believed or portrayed by biographers. His personal acquaintance with so many authors around the world also contributed to the wide extent of his reading. References are cited after each title below.

Adventures of Captain Bonneville, by Washington Irving (Gribben, p. 346)

Adventures of Don Quixote, by Miguel de Cervantes (Emerson, p. 8)

Adventures of Sherlock Holmes, by Sir Arthur Conan Doyle (Gribben, p. 201)

The Age of Reason, by Thomas Paine (Emerson, p. 8)

Alice's Adventures in Wonderland, by Lewis Carroll (pseudo. Charles Dodgson), (Gribben, p. 198)

An *American Dictionary of the English Language*, by Noah Webster (Gribben, p. 753)

American Notes for General Circulation, by Charles Dickens (Gribben, p. 187)

"An Old Fogey," (story) by Max Adeler (Emerson, p. 175)

Anne of Green Gables, by Lucy Maud Montgomery (Gribben, p. 480)

Antony and Cleopatra, by William Shakespeare (Gribben, p. 623)

Arabian Nights (Gribben, p. 26)

As You Like It, by William Shakespeare (Gribben, p. 623)

Atlantic Essays, by Thomas Wentworth Higginson (Gribben, p. 313)

The Atlantic Monthly Magazine (Gribben, p. 30 and Howells, p. 3)

"Aurora Leigh," (poem) by Elizabeth Barrett Browning (Harris,p. 130)

The Autocrat of the Breakfast-Table, by Oliver Wendell Holmes (Gribben, p. 317)

Barnaby Rudge, by Charles Dickens (Gribben, p. 187)

The Bible (Gribben, p. 63)

The Boy's King Arthur, by Sir Thomas Malory (Gribben, p. 447)

Browning, Robert, extensive poems (Gribben, p. 91)

The Canterbury Tales, by Geoffrey Chaucer (Gribben, p. 139)

Century Magazine (Gribben, p. 135)

The Christian Science Journal (Gribben, p. 141)

A Christmas Carol, by Charles Dickens (Gribben, p. 188)

The Citizen of the World, by Oliver Goldsmith (Emerson, p. 8 and Gribben, p. 265)

The Comedy of Errors, by William Shakespeare (Gribben, p. 623)

"The Complaint: or Night Thoughts on Life, Death, and Immortality," (poem) by Edward Young (Harris, p. 130)

The Count of Monte-Cristo, by Alexandre Dumas (Gribben, p. 206)

Cranford, by Elizabeth Gaskell (Gribben, p. 253)

Critique of Pure Reason, by Immanuel Kant (Gribben, p. 363)

Cuchulain of Muirthemne: The Story of the Men of the Red Branch of Ulster, by Lady Gregory (Gribben, p. 277)

Cymbeline, by William Shakespeare (Gribben, p. 623)

A Daughter of Russia, by Ivan Turgenev (Gribben, p. 719)

David Copperfield, by Charles Dickens (Gribben, p. 188)

The Decameron or Ten Days' Entertainment of Boccaccio, by Giovanni Boccaccio (Gribben, p.76)

Democracy in America, by Alexis de Tocqueville (Gribben, p. 706)

The Descent of Man, by Charles Darwin (Gribben, p. 174)

The Dialogues of Plato, by Plato (Gribben, p. 549)

The Diary of Samuel Pepys, by Samuel Pepys (Gribben, p. 539)

The Divine Comedy, by Alighieri Dante (Gribben, p. 173)

Dombey and Son, by Charles Dickens (Harris, p. 108)

Dracula, by Bram Stoker (Gribben, p. 668)

The Ecclesiastical History of New-England from Its First Planting... unto... 1698, by Cotton Mather (Gribben, p. 457)

Elements of Geology, J.L. Comstock (Gribben, p. 156)

Encyclopedia Britannica: A Dictionary of Arts, Sciences, and General Literature (Gribben, p. 222)

English Humorists of the Eighteenth Century, by William Thackeray (esp. essay on Swift) (Harris, p. 133)

Essay on Criticism, by Alexander Pope (Gribben, p. 554)

Essay on Man, by Alexander Pope (Gribben, p. 554)

Essays, Ralph Waldo Emerson (Gribben, p. 221)

Exploration of the Valley of the Amazon, U.S. Navy Report, (Kaplan, p. 57)

The Faerie Queen, by Edmund Spencer (Gribben, p. 654)

Far From the Madding Crowd, by Thomas Hardy (Gribben, p. 292)

Fate of the Children of Uisneach... with Translation, Notes, and a Complete Vocabulary, by Lady Gregory (Gribben, p. 278)

Faust, by Johann Wolfgang von Goethe (Gribben, p. 263)

Five Weeks in a Balloon, by Jules Verne (Gribben, p. 725)

Frankenstein, by Mary Shelley (Gribben, p. 639)

Freedom of Will, by Jonathan Edwards (Gribben, p. 214)

The French Revolution, by Thomas Carlyle (Fulton, p. 175 and Harris, p. 130)

The Gates Ajar, by Elizabeth Stuart Phelps (Gribben, p. 741)

"Gettysburg Address," (speech) by Abraham Lincoln (Gribben, p. 410)

Great Expectations, by Charles Dickens (Gribben, p. 189)

Gulliver's Travels, by Jonathan Swift (Gribben, p. 679)

Hamlet, by William Shakespeare (Gribben, p. 623)

Hannibal Courier (newspaper) (Emerson, p. 3)

Harper's Monthly Magazine (Gribben, p. 293)

Harte, Bret, several works (Gribben, p. 297)

The Heavenly Twins, by Sarah Grand (Gribben, p. 270)

Hedda Gabler, by Henrik Ibsen (Gribben, p. 343)

Henry V, by William Shakespeare (Gribben, p. 625)

The History of England From the Accession of James II, by Thomas Babington Macaulay (Fulton, p. 123)

A History of England in the Eighteenth Century, by William Lecky (Fulton, p. 133)

History of the Rise and Influence of the Spirit of Rationalism in Europe (2 vol.), by William Lecky (Fulton, p. 105)

The House of Mirth, by Edith Wharton (Gribben, p. 758)

The House of the Seven Gables, by Nathaniel Hawthorne (Gribben, p. 301)

Howells, William Dean, several works (Gribben, p. 326)

The Idylls of the King, by Alfred Lord Tennyson (Gribben, p. 693)

The Iliad and *The Odyssey*, by Homer (Gribben, p. 320)

The Independent (periodical) (Gribben, p. 343)

Ivan the Fool, by Leo Tolstoi (Gribben, p. 706)

Ivanhoe, by Sir Walter Scott (Gribben, p. 615)

Jude the Obscure, by Thomas Hardy (Gribben, p. 292)

Julius Caesar, by William Shakespeare (Emerson, p. 8)

The Jungle, by Upton Sinclair (Gribben, p. 644)

Kidnapped, by Robert Louis Stevenson (Gribben, p. 664)

King Lear, by William Shakespeare (Gribben, p. 627)

Kipling, Rudyard, *The Jungle Book*, *Kim*, and several other works (Gribben, p. 375)

The Koran: Commonly Called the Alkoran of Mohammed (Gribben, p. 388)

Last Verses, by Sarah Chauncey Woolsey (pseudo. Susan Coolidge) (Gribben, p. 786)

Leather-Stocking Tales, James Fenimore Cooper (Gribben, p. 160)

Leaves of Grass, Walt Whitman (Gribben, p. 764)

Les Misérables, by Victor Hugo (Gribben, p. 339)

Letters of Samuel Johnson, by Samuel Johnson (Gribben, p. 356)

Life is Worth Living, and Other Stories, by Leo Tolstoi (Gribben, p. 707)

The Life of Benjamin Franklin, Written by Himself, by Benjamin Franklin (Gribben, p. 241)

The Life of Samuel Johnson, by James Boswell (Gribben, p. 78)

Little Dorritt, Charles Dickens, (Emerson, p. 8 and Gribben, p. 189)

London Times (newspaper), (Gribben, p. 418)

Looking Backward, 2000–1887, by Edward Bellamy (Howells, p. 43 and Gribben, p. 58)

MacBeth, by William Shakespeare (Gribben, p. 627)

The Maine Woods, by Henry David Thoreau (Gribben, p. 703)

Major Jones's Sketches of Travel, by William Tappan Thompson (Emerson, p. 8)

"The Man Without a Country," (story) by Edward Everett Hale (Gribben, p. 285)

The Marble Faun, by Nathaniel Hawthorne (Gribben, p. 301)

Martin Chuzzlewit, by Charles Dickens (Gribben, p. 190)

The Merchant of Venice, by William Shakespeare (Harris, p. 124)

The Merry Adventures of Robin Hood of Great Renown, by Howard Pyle (Gribben, p. 563)

The Merry Wives of Windsor, by William Shakespeare (Gribben, p. 629)

Middlemarch, by George Eliot (Gribben, p. 217)

A Midsummer Night's Dream, by William Shakespeare (Gribben, p. 629)

"Mrs. George Christopher Riggs," (story) by Kate Douglas Wiggin (Gribben, p. 768)

Much Ado About Nothing, by William Shakespeare (Gribben, p. 629)

Murders of the Rue Morgue and Other Tales, by Edgar Allan Poe (Gribben, p. 552)

New York Times (newspaper) (Gribben, p. 505)

Nicholas Nickleby, by Charles Dickens (Gribben, p. 192)

Nick of the Woods, by Robert Montgomery Bird (Emerson, p. 12)

The Old Curiosity Shop, by Charles Dickens (Gribben, p. 192)

Oliver Twist, by Charles Dickens (Gribben, p. 190)

On the Origin of the Species, by Charles Darwin (Gribben, p. 176)

Othello, by William Shakespeare (Gribben, p. 628)

Our Mutual Friend, by Charles Dickens (Gribben, p. 190)
Paradise Lost, by John Milton (Gribben, p. 476)
Personal Memoirs of U.S. Grant, by Ulysses S. Grant (Gribben, p. 272)
Peter Parley's Magazine (children's) (Paine, p. 14)
Philadelphia as It Is in 1852, by R.A. Smith (Emerson, p. 7)
Picciola, by Joseph Xavier Boniface Saintine (Gribben, p. 598)
Pickwick Papers, Charles Dickens (Emerson, p. 37 and Gribben, p. 191)
Pilgrim's Progress, by John Bunyan (Gribben, p. 111)
The Poetical Works of Alfred, Lord Tennyson, by Alfred, Lord Tennyson (Gribben, p. 694)
Poets and Dreamers: Studies and Translations from the Irish, by Lady Gregory (Gribben, p. 278)
Potiphar Papers, by George W. Curtis (Emerson, p. 8)
Pride and Prejudice, by Jane Austen (Gribben, p. 32)
Richard III, by William Shakespeare (Gribben, p. 630)
Rime of the Ancient Mariner, by Samuel Taylor Coleridge (Gribben, p. 152)
"Rip Van Winkle," (story) by Washing Irving (Gribben, p. 346)
Rise of the Dutch Republic (3 volumes), by John Motley (Harris, p. 129)
Robinson Crusoe, by Daniel Defoe (Gribben, p. 180)
Romeo and Juliet, by William Shakespeare (Gribben, p. 631)
The Scarlet Letter, A Romance, by Nathaniel Hawthorne (Gribben, p. 302)
Sense and Sensibility, by Jane Austen (Gribben, p. 34)
Shelley, Percy Bysshe, several poems (Gribben, p. 640)
Sir Guy of the Dolorus Blast, by William Morris (Howells, p. 16)
The Song of Hiawatha, by Henry Wadsworth Longfellow (Gribben, p. 419)
Stories of Red Hanrahan, by William Butler Yeats (Gribben, p. 790)
The Story of My Life, by Helen Keller (Gribben, p. 365)
A Tale of Two Cities, by Charles Dickens (Gribben, p. 192)
The Taming of the Shrew, by William Shakespeare (Gribben, p. 631)
The Tempest, by William Shakespeare (Gribben, p. 631)
Through the Looking-Glass and What Alice Found There, by Lewis Carroll (pseud. Charles Dodgson), (Gribben, p. 198)
Tom Brown's School Days, by Thomas Hughes (Gribben, p. 338)

Tom Jones, by Henry Fielding (Gribben, p. 229)

Treasure Island, by Robert Louis Stevenson (Gribben, p. 664)

Twenty Thousand Leagues Under the Sea, by Jules Verne (Gribben, p. 727)

The Two Gentlemen of Verona, by William Shakespeare (Gribben, p. 632)

Two Years Before the Mast: A Personal Narrative, by Richard Henry Dana (Gribben, p. 171)

Uncle Remus: His Songs and His Sayings, The Folk-Lore of the Old Plantation, by Joel Chandler Harris (Gribben, p. 295)

Uncle Tom's Cabin, by Harriet Beecher Stowe (Gribben, p. 672)

Venus and Adonis, by William Shakespeare (Gribben, p. 632)

Wordsworth, William, several poems (Gribben, p. 786)

The Works of Charles Lamb, by Charles Lamb (Gribben, p. 393)

The Youth's Companion (children's magazine) (Gribben, p. 795)

Appendix C

QUOTABLE TWAIN

Mark Twain was famous for his maxims that he told in lecture tours and speeches and in his published writing, personal correspondence, and notebooks. He was so famous for quotations that today there are even some that are commonly attributed to him that scholars cannot authenticate Samuel Clemens actually said or wrote.

The maxims below are followed by citations of where they can be found in Clemens's writing.

"I believe that our Heavenly Father invented man because he was disappointed in the monkey." (*The Autobiography of Mark Twain*, chapter 57)

"Adam and Eve had many advantages, but the principal one was that they escaped teething." (*Pudd'nhead Wilson*, chapter 4)

"Let us endeavor so to live that when we come to die even the undertaker will be sorry." (*Pudd'nhead Wilson*, chapter 6)

"One of the most striking differences between a cat and a lie is that a cat has only nine lives." (*Pudd'nhead Wilson*, chapter 7)

"The holy passion of Friendship is of so sweet and steady and loyal and enduring a nature that it will last through a whole lifetime if not asked to lend money." (*Pudd'nhead Wilson*, chapter 8)

"Reader, suppose you were an idiot. And suppose you were a member of Congress. But I repeat myself." (Draft manuscript, *Mark Twain: A Biography*)

"October. This is one of the peculiarly dangerous months to speculate in stocks in. The others are July, January, September, April, November,

May, March, June, December, August, and February." (*Pudd'nhead Wilson*, Conclusion)

"Nothing so needs reforming as other people's habits." (*Pudd'nhead Wilson*, chapter 15)

"Behold, the fool saith, 'Put not all thine eggs in the one basket'—which is but a manner of saying, 'Scatter your money and your attention': but the wise man saith, 'Put all your eggs in the one basket and—WATCH THAT BASKET.'" (*Pudd'nhead Wilson*, chapter 15)

"If you pick up a starving dog and make him prosperous, he will not bite you. This is the principal difference between a dog and a man." (*Pudd'nhead Wilson*, chapter 16)

"April 1. This is the day upon which we are reminded of what we are on the other three hundred and sixty-four." (*Pudd'nhead Wilson*, chapter 21)

"October 12, the Discovery. It was wonderful to find America, but it would have been more wonderful to miss it." (*Pudd'nhead Wilson*, Conclusion)

"Ah, well, I am a great & sublime fool. But then I am God's fool, & all His works must be contemplated with respect." (Letter to William Dean Howells, c. December 28, 1877)

"Be good and you will be lonesome." (*Following the Equator*, flyleaf)

"I don't know of a single foreign product that enters this country untaxed except the answer to prayer." (*Mark Twain's Speeches*, p. 398)

"It is curious—curious that physical courage should be so common in the world, and moral courage so rare." (*Mark Twain in Eruption*, p. 69).

Appendix D

BOOKS BY MARK TWAIN

The chronological listing of book publications below includes those published both in the United States and England during Samuel Clemens's lifetime. This helpful, straightforward listing from Clemens's vast and complicated publication history is derived from the guide, *Mark Twain A–Z, The Essential Reference to His Life and Writings*, by R. Kent Rasmussen. Posthumous publications of previously unpublished or uncollected material by the author have appeared as late as 1995.

1867 *The Celebrated Jumping Frog of Calaveras County and Other Sketches*. New York: C. H. Webb.

1869 *The Innocents Abroad, or The New Pilgrims' Progress; Being Some Account of the Steamship Quaker City's Pleasure Excursion to Europe and the Holy Land*. Hartford, Conn.: American Publishing Company.

1871 *Eye Openers*. London: John Camden Hotten.

1871 *Mark Twain's (Burlesque) Autobiography and First Romance*. New York: Shelden.

1872 *Screamers*. London: John Camden Hotten.

1873 *Choice Humorous Works of Mark Twain*. London: John Camden Hotten.

1874 *The Gilded Age: A Tale of To-day*. Hartford, Conn.: American Publishing Company. Co-authored with Charles Dudley Warner.

1875 *Sketches, New and Old*. Hartford, Conn.: American Publishing Company.

1876 *The Adventures of Tom Sawyer*. Hartford, Conn.: American Publishing Company. (Published in England a few weeks before).

1877 *A True Story and the Recent Carnival of Crime*. Boston: James R. Osgood.

1878 *Punch, Brothers, Punch! and Other Sketches*. New York: Slote, Woodman.

1880 *A Tramp Abroad*. Hartford, Conn.: American Publishing Company.

1880 *[Date, 1601] Conversation as It Was by the Social Fireside in the Time of the Tudors* [privately published in different editions under various titles].

1881 *The Prince and the Pauper: A Tale for Young People of All Ages*. Boston: James R. Osgood.

1882 *The Stolen White Elephant, Etc*. Boston: James R. Osgood.

1883 *Life on the Mississippi*. Boston: James R. Osgood.

1885 *Adventures of Huckleberry Finn*. New York: Charles L. Webster. [inaugural publication of Clemens's publishing company, Webster; published in England in late 1884.]

1889 *A Connecticut Yankee in King Arthur's Court*. New York: Charles L. Webster.

1892 *Merry Tales*. New York: Charles L. Webster.

1892 *The American Claimant*. New York: Charles L. Webster.

1893 *The £1,000,000 Bank-Note and Other New Stories*. New York: Charles L. Webster.

1894 *Tom Sawyer Abroad*. New York: Charles L. Webster.

1894 *Pudd'nhead Wilson and Those Extraordinary Twins*. Hartford, Conn.: American Publishing Company.

1896 *Tom Sawyer Abroad; Tom Sawyer, Detective and Other Stories*. New York: Harper.

1896 *Personal Recollections of Joan of Arc*. New York: Harper.

1897 *How to Tell a Story and Other Essays*. New York: Harper.

1897 *Following the Equator: A Journey Around the World*. Hartford, Conn.: American Publishing Company.

1898 *More Tramps Abroad*. London: Chatto and Windus.

1899 *The American Claimant and Other Stories and Sketches*. New York: Harper.

1899 *Literary Essays*. New York: Harper.

1900 *English As She Is Taught*. Boston: Mutual Book Company.

The Man That Corrupted Hadleyburg and Other Stories and Essays. New York: Harper.

1902 *A Double-Barrelled Detective Story*. New York: Harper.

1903 *My Début as a Literary Person and Other Essays and Stories*. Hartford, Conn.: American Publishing Company.

1904 *A Dog's Tale*. New York: Harper.

1904 *Extracts from Adam's Diary*. New York: Harper.

1905 *King Leopold's Soliloquy: A Defense of His Congo Rule*. Boston: P.R. Warren.

1906 *Eve's Diary*. New York: Harper.

1906 *What Is Man?* New York: De Vinne Press.

1906 *The $30,000 Bequest and Other Stories*. New York: Harper.

1907 *Christian Science*. New York: Harper.

1907 *A Horse's Tale*. New York and London: Harper.

1909 *Is Shakespeare Dead? from My Autobiography*. New York: Harper.

1909 *Extract from Captain Stormfield's Visit to Heaven*. New York: Harper.

Appendix E

IMPORTANT PLACES AND HOLDINGS IN MARK TWAIN STUDIES

Mark Twain Birthplace State Historic Site
37352 Shrine Road
Florida, MO 65283
(573) 565-3449
Website: http://www.mostateparks.com/twainsite.htm

Mark Twain Boyhood Home and Museum
208 Hill Street
Hannibal, MO 63401-3316
(573) 221-7975
Website: http://www.marktwainmuseum.org/

The Center for Mark Twain Studies at Quarry Farm
One Park Place
Elmira, NY 14901
(607) 735-1941
Website: http://www.elmira.edu/academics/ar_marktwain.shtml

The Mark Twain House
351 Farmington Avenue
Hartford, CT 06105
(860) 247-0998, ext. 26
Website: http://www.marktwainhouse.org/

The Mark Twain Room
Buffalo & Erie County Public Library
1 Lafayette Square

Buffalo, NY 14203
(716) 858-8900
Website:
http://www.buffalolib.org/libraries/collections/index.asp?sec = twain

Mark Twain Papers
University of California at Berkeley
480 Doe Library
Berkeley, CA 947200-6000
(510) 642-6480
Website: http://bancroft.berkeley.edu/MTP/

BIBLIOGRAPHY

SELECTED WORKS AND EDITIONS OF MARK TWAIN

Twain, Mark [Samuel Langhorne Clemens]. *Adventures of Huckleberry Finn* [1885]. Berkeley: University of California Press, Mark Twain Library, 1985.

———. *The Adventures of Tom Sawyer* [1876], Edited by John C. Gerber and Paul Baender. Berkeley: University of California Press, 1982.

———. *The American Claimant and Other Stories and Sketches*. 1897. Reprint, New York: Harper and Brothers, 1899.

———. *The Autobiography of Mark Twain, Including Chapters Now Published for the First Time*. Edited by Charles Neider. New York: Harper & Row, 1959.

———. *Christian Science*. New York: Harper and Brothers, 1907.

———. *Clemens of the Call: Mark Twain in San Francisco*. Edited by Edgar M. Branch. Berkeley: University of California Press, 1969. [Selected articles Twain wrote for the *San Francisco Call* in 1864.]

———. *Collected Tales, Sketches, Speeches, and Essays, 1852–1890*. Edited by Louis J. Budd. New York: Library of America, 1992.

———. *Collected Tales, Sketches, Speeches, and Essays, 1891–1910*. Edited by Louis J. Budd. New York: Library of America, 1992.

———. *A Connecticut Yankee in King Arthur's Court* [1889]. Edited by Bernard Stein. Berkeley: University of California Press, 1983.

———. *A Dog's Tale*. New York: Harper & Brothers, 1904.

———. *A Double-Barrelled Detective Story*. New York: Harper & Brothers, 1902.

———. *Early Tales and Sketches, Vol. 1, 1851–1864*. Edited by Edgar Marquess Branch and Robert H. Hirst. Berkeley: University of California Press, 1979.

———. *English As She Is Taught*. 1900. Ann Arbor, Mich.: Allegany Press, 1998.

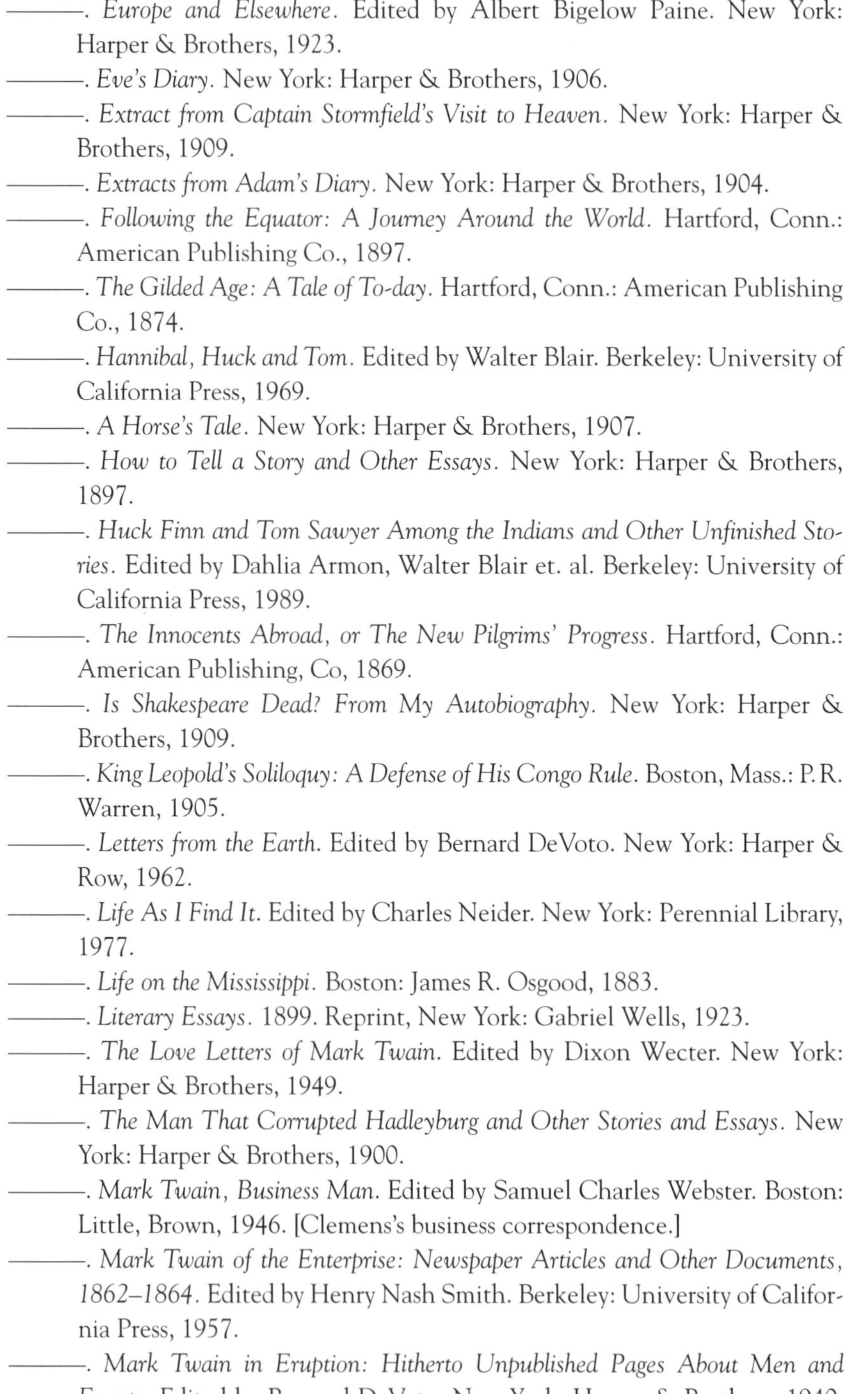

———. *Europe and Elsewhere*. Edited by Albert Bigelow Paine. New York: Harper & Brothers, 1923.

———. *Eve's Diary*. New York: Harper & Brothers, 1906.

———. *Extract from Captain Stormfield's Visit to Heaven*. New York: Harper & Brothers, 1909.

———. *Extracts from Adam's Diary*. New York: Harper & Brothers, 1904.

———. *Following the Equator: A Journey Around the World*. Hartford, Conn.: American Publishing Co., 1897.

———. *The Gilded Age: A Tale of To-day*. Hartford, Conn.: American Publishing Co., 1874.

———. *Hannibal, Huck and Tom*. Edited by Walter Blair. Berkeley: University of California Press, 1969.

———. *A Horse's Tale*. New York: Harper & Brothers, 1907.

———. *How to Tell a Story and Other Essays*. New York: Harper & Brothers, 1897.

———. *Huck Finn and Tom Sawyer Among the Indians and Other Unfinished Stories*. Edited by Dahlia Armon, Walter Blair et. al. Berkeley: University of California Press, 1989.

———. *The Innocents Abroad, or The New Pilgrims' Progress*. Hartford, Conn.: American Publishing, Co, 1869.

———. *Is Shakespeare Dead? From My Autobiography*. New York: Harper & Brothers, 1909.

———. *King Leopold's Soliloquy: A Defense of His Congo Rule*. Boston, Mass.: P.R. Warren, 1905.

———. *Letters from the Earth*. Edited by Bernard DeVoto. New York: Harper & Row, 1962.

———. *Life As I Find It*. Edited by Charles Neider. New York: Perennial Library, 1977.

———. *Life on the Mississippi*. Boston: James R. Osgood, 1883.

———. *Literary Essays*. 1899. Reprint, New York: Gabriel Wells, 1923.

———. *The Love Letters of Mark Twain*. Edited by Dixon Wecter. New York: Harper & Brothers, 1949.

———. *The Man That Corrupted Hadleyburg and Other Stories and Essays*. New York: Harper & Brothers, 1900.

———. *Mark Twain, Business Man*. Edited by Samuel Charles Webster. Boston: Little, Brown, 1946. [Clemens's business correspondence.]

———. *Mark Twain of the Enterprise: Newspaper Articles and Other Documents, 1862–1864*. Edited by Henry Nash Smith. Berkeley: University of California Press, 1957.

———. *Mark Twain in Eruption: Hitherto Unpublished Pages About Men and Events*. Edited by Bernard DeVoto. New York: Harper & Brothers, 1940.

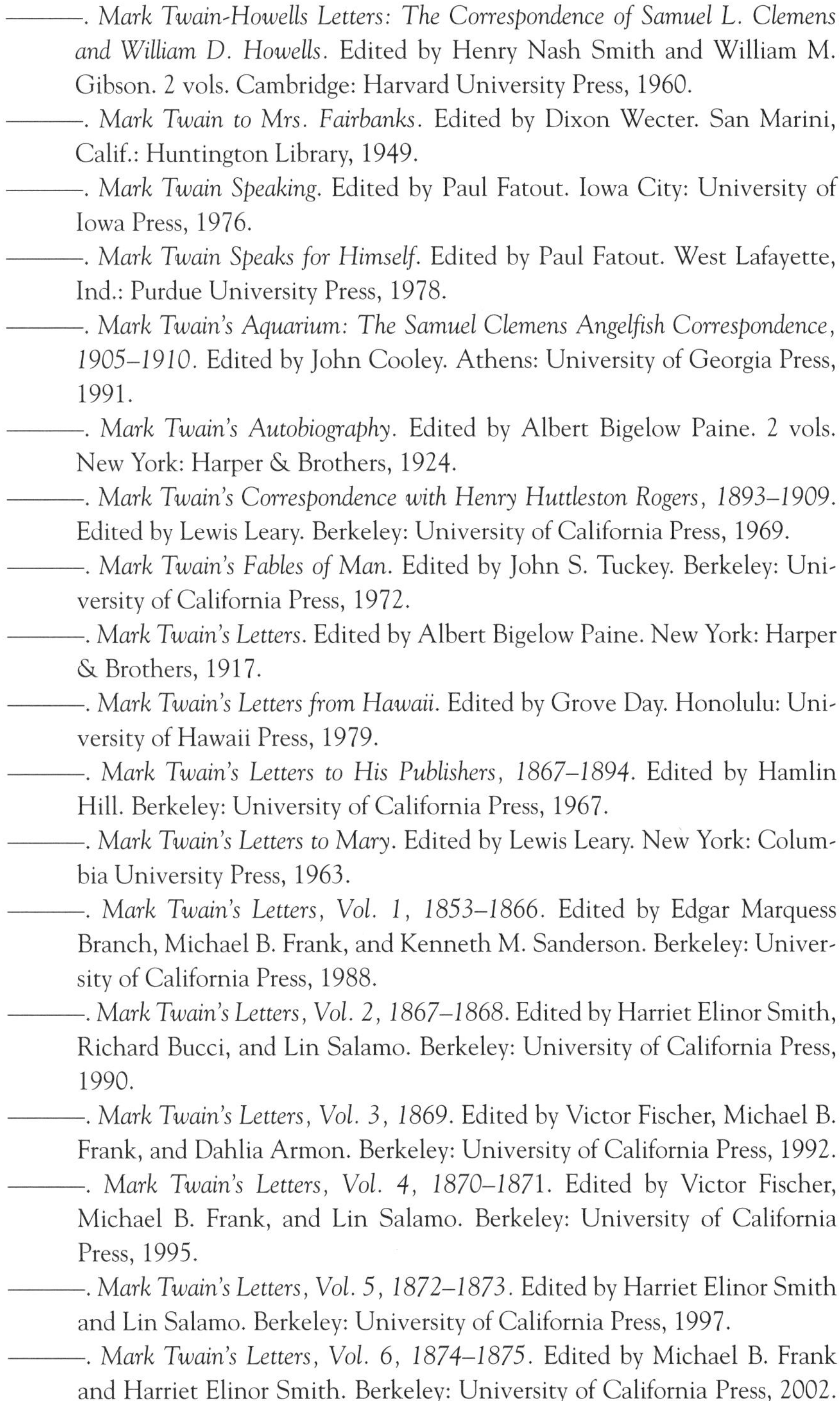

———. *Mark Twain-Howells Letters: The Correspondence of Samuel L. Clemens and William D. Howells*. Edited by Henry Nash Smith and William M. Gibson. 2 vols. Cambridge: Harvard University Press, 1960.

———. *Mark Twain to Mrs. Fairbanks*. Edited by Dixon Wecter. San Marini, Calif.: Huntington Library, 1949.

———. *Mark Twain Speaking*. Edited by Paul Fatout. Iowa City: University of Iowa Press, 1976.

———. *Mark Twain Speaks for Himself*. Edited by Paul Fatout. West Lafayette, Ind.: Purdue University Press, 1978.

———. *Mark Twain's Aquarium: The Samuel Clemens Angelfish Correspondence, 1905–1910*. Edited by John Cooley. Athens: University of Georgia Press, 1991.

———. *Mark Twain's Autobiography*. Edited by Albert Bigelow Paine. 2 vols. New York: Harper & Brothers, 1924.

———. *Mark Twain's Correspondence with Henry Huttleston Rogers, 1893–1909*. Edited by Lewis Leary. Berkeley: University of California Press, 1969.

———. *Mark Twain's Fables of Man*. Edited by John S. Tuckey. Berkeley: University of California Press, 1972.

———. *Mark Twain's Letters*. Edited by Albert Bigelow Paine. New York: Harper & Brothers, 1917.

———. *Mark Twain's Letters from Hawaii*. Edited by Grove Day. Honolulu: University of Hawaii Press, 1979.

———. *Mark Twain's Letters to His Publishers, 1867–1894*. Edited by Hamlin Hill. Berkeley: University of California Press, 1967.

———. *Mark Twain's Letters to Mary*. Edited by Lewis Leary. New York: Columbia University Press, 1963.

———. *Mark Twain's Letters, Vol. 1, 1853–1866*. Edited by Edgar Marquess Branch, Michael B. Frank, and Kenneth M. Sanderson. Berkeley: University of California Press, 1988.

———. *Mark Twain's Letters, Vol. 2, 1867–1868*. Edited by Harriet Elinor Smith, Richard Bucci, and Lin Salamo. Berkeley: University of California Press, 1990.

———. *Mark Twain's Letters, Vol. 3, 1869*. Edited by Victor Fischer, Michael B. Frank, and Dahlia Armon. Berkeley: University of California Press, 1992.

———. *Mark Twain's Letters, Vol. 4, 1870–1871*. Edited by Victor Fischer, Michael B. Frank, and Lin Salamo. Berkeley: University of California Press, 1995.

———. *Mark Twain's Letters, Vol. 5, 1872–1873*. Edited by Harriet Elinor Smith and Lin Salamo. Berkeley: University of California Press, 1997.

———. *Mark Twain's Letters, Vol. 6, 1874–1875*. Edited by Michael B. Frank and Harriet Elinor Smith. Berkeley: University of California Press, 2002.

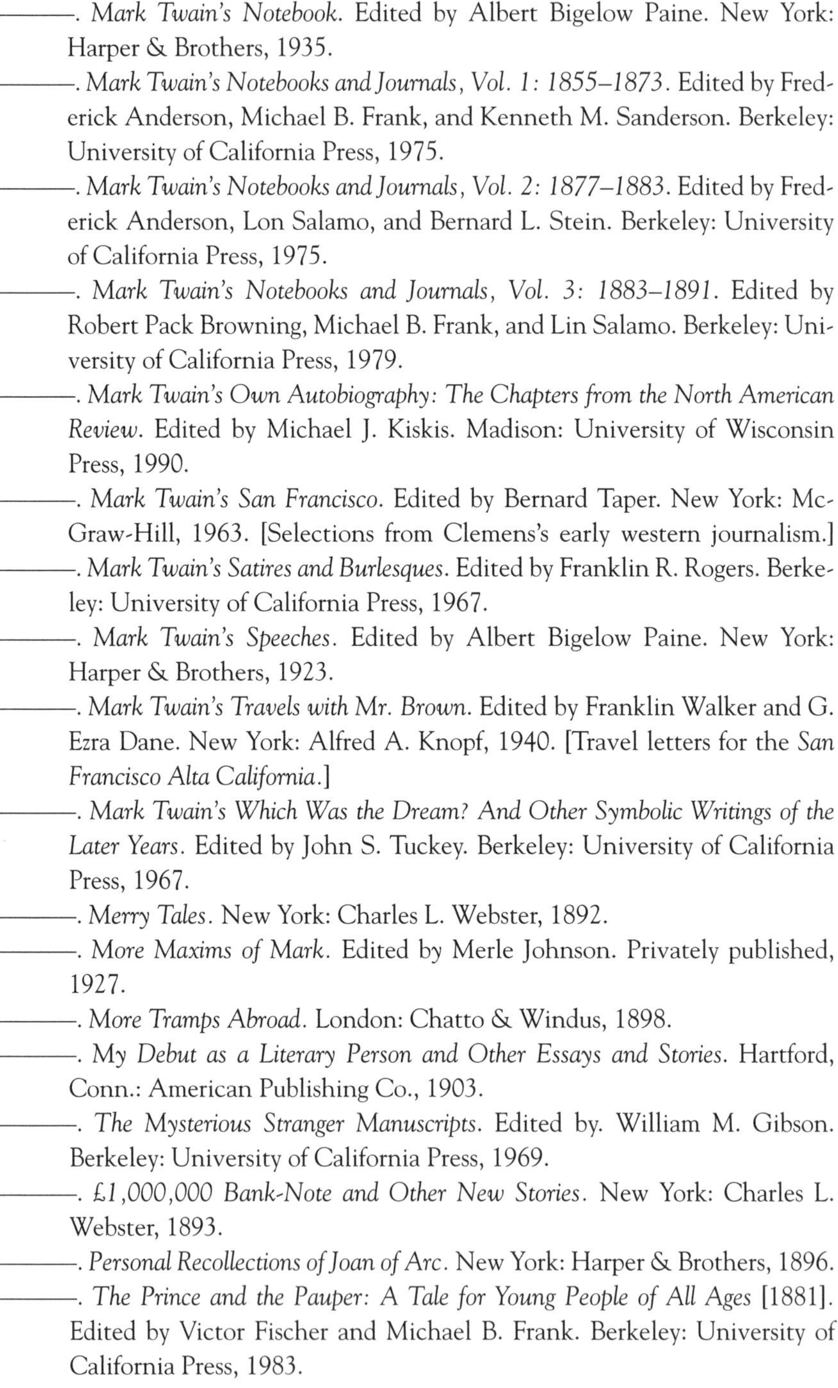

———. *Mark Twain's Notebook*. Edited by Albert Bigelow Paine. New York: Harper & Brothers, 1935.

———. *Mark Twain's Notebooks and Journals, Vol. 1: 1855–1873*. Edited by Frederick Anderson, Michael B. Frank, and Kenneth M. Sanderson. Berkeley: University of California Press, 1975.

———. *Mark Twain's Notebooks and Journals, Vol. 2: 1877–1883*. Edited by Frederick Anderson, Lon Salamo, and Bernard L. Stein. Berkeley: University of California Press, 1975.

———. *Mark Twain's Notebooks and Journals, Vol. 3: 1883–1891*. Edited by Robert Pack Browning, Michael B. Frank, and Lin Salamo. Berkeley: University of California Press, 1979.

———. *Mark Twain's Own Autobiography: The Chapters from the North American Review*. Edited by Michael J. Kiskis. Madison: University of Wisconsin Press, 1990.

———. *Mark Twain's San Francisco*. Edited by Bernard Taper. New York: McGraw-Hill, 1963. [Selections from Clemens's early western journalism.]

———. *Mark Twain's Satires and Burlesques*. Edited by Franklin R. Rogers. Berkeley: University of California Press, 1967.

———. *Mark Twain's Speeches*. Edited by Albert Bigelow Paine. New York: Harper & Brothers, 1923.

———. *Mark Twain's Travels with Mr. Brown*. Edited by Franklin Walker and G. Ezra Dane. New York: Alfred A. Knopf, 1940. [Travel letters for the *San Francisco Alta California*.]

———. *Mark Twain's Which Was the Dream? And Other Symbolic Writings of the Later Years*. Edited by John S. Tuckey. Berkeley: University of California Press, 1967.

———. *Merry Tales*. New York: Charles L. Webster, 1892.

———. *More Maxims of Mark*. Edited by Merle Johnson. Privately published, 1927.

———. *More Tramps Abroad*. London: Chatto & Windus, 1898.

———. My *Debut as a Literary Person and Other Essays and Stories*. Hartford, Conn.: American Publishing Co., 1903.

———. *The Mysterious Stranger Manuscripts*. Edited by. William M. Gibson. Berkeley: University of California Press, 1969.

———. *£1,000,000 Bank-Note and Other New Stories*. New York: Charles L. Webster, 1893.

———. *Personal Recollections of Joan of Arc*. New York: Harper & Brothers, 1896.

———. *The Prince and the Pauper: A Tale for Young People of All Ages* [1881]. Edited by Victor Fischer and Michael B. Frank. Berkeley: University of California Press, 1983.

———. *Pudd'nhead Wilson and Those Extraordinary Twins.* Hartford, Conn.: American Publishing Co., 1894.

———. *Roughing It* [1872]. Edited by Edited by Harriet Elinor Smith, Edgar Marquess Branch, Lin Salamo, and Robert Pack Browning. Berkeley: University of California Press, 1995.

———. *The Stolen White Elephant, Etc.* Boston: James R. Osgood, 1882.

———. *The $30,000 Bequest and Other Stories.* New York: Harper & Brothers, 1906.

———. *Tom Sawyer Abroad; Tom Sawyer, Detective* [1894; 1896]. Edited by John C. Gerber and Terry Firkins. Berkeley: University of California Press, 1982.

———. *A Tramp Abroad.* Hartford, Conn.: American Publishing Co., 1880.

———. *Traveling with the Innocents Abroad: Mark Twain's Original Reports from Europe and the Holy Land.* Edited by. Daniel Morley McKeithan. Norman, Okla.: University of Oklahoma Press, 1958.

———. *Twins of Genius.* Edited by. Guy Cardwell. London: Neville Spearman, 1962. [Correspondence with George Washington Cable.]

———. *What Is Man? And Other Philosophical Writings.* Edited by Paul Baender. Berkeley: University of California Press, 1973.

SECONDARY SOURCES

Anderson, Frederick, and Kenneth M. Sanderson, eds. *Mark Twain: The Critical Heritage.* London: Routledge and Kegan Paul, 1971.

Andrews, Kenneth R. *Nook Farm: Mark Twain's Hartford Circle.* Cambridge: Harvard University Press, 1950.

Arac, Jonathan. *Huckleberry Finn and Idol and Target: The Functions of Criticism in Our Time.* Madison: University of Wisconsin Press, 1997.

Baetzhold, Howard G. *Mark Twain and John Bull: The British Connection.* Bloomington: Indiana University Press, 1970.

Beaver, Harold, *Huckleberry Finn.* London: Unwin Hyman, 1988.

Berret, Anthony J. *Mark Twain and Shakespeare: A Cultural Legacy.* Lanham, Md.: University Press of America, 1993.

Blair, Walter. *Mark Twain and Huck Finn.* Berkeley: University of California Press, 1960.

Bloom, Harold, ed. *Mark Twain.* New York: Chelsea House, 1986.

Branch, Edgar. *The Literary Apprenticeship of Mark Twain.* Iowa City: University Press of Iowa, 1950.

Bridgman, Richard. *Traveling in Mark Twain.* Berkeley: University of California Press, 1987.

Budd, Louis J. *Mark Twain: The Contemporary Reviews*. Cambridge: Cambridge University Press, 1999.

———. *Mark Twain: Social Philosopher*. Bloomington: Indiana University Press, 1962.

———. *Our Mark Twain: The Making of His Public Personality*. Philadelphia: University of Pennsylvania Press, 1983.

———. "Overbooking Halley's Comet," Online. Available: http://www.citadel.edu/faculty/leonard/budd.htm. (accessed: 14 October 2003).

———, ed. *Critical Essays on Mark Twain, 1867–1910*. Boston: G.K. Hall, 1982.

———, ed. *Critical Essays on Mark Twain, 1910–1980*. Boston: G.K. Hall, 1983.

———, ed. *New Essays on "Adventures of Huckleberry Finn."* Cambridge: Cambridge University Press, 1985.

Budd, Louis J., and Edwin H. Cady, eds. *On Mark Twain: The Best from American Literature*. Durham, N.C.: Duke University Press, 1987.

Camfield, Gregg. *Sentimental Twain: Samuel Clemens in the Maze of Moral Philosophy*. Philadelphia: University of Pennsylvania Press, 1994.

Cardwell, Guy. *The Man Who Was Mark Twain: Images and Ideologies*. New Haven: Yale University Press, 1991.

———. *Twins of Genius*. East Lansing: Michigan State College Press, 1953.

Chadwick-Joshua, Jocelyn. *The Jim Dilemma: Reading Race in Huckleberry Finn*. Jackson: University Press of Mississippi, 1998.

Champion, Laurie, ed. *The Critical Response to Mark Twain's "Huckleberry Finn."* Westport, Conn.: Greenwood Press, 1991.

Clemens, Clara. *My Father Mark Twain*. New York: Harper & Brothers, 1931.

Clemens, Susy. *Papa: An Intimate Biography of Mark Twain by His Thirteen-Year-Old Daughter Susy, with a forword and commentary by her father*. Edited by Charles Neider. Garden City, N.Y.: Doubleday, 1985.

Covici, Pascal Jr. *Humor and Revolution in American Literature: The Puritan Connection*. Columbia: University of Missouri Press, 1997.

———. *Mark Twain's Humor: The Image of a World*. Dallas: Southern Methodist University Press, 1962.

Cox, James M. *Mark Twain: The Fate of Humor*. Princeton, N.J.: Princeton University Press, 1966.

David, Beverly R. *Mark Twain and His Illustrators*, 2 vols. (1869–1875). Troy, N.Y.: Whitson, 1986.

Davis, Sara deSaussure, and Philip D. Beidler, eds. *The Mythologizing of Mark Twain*. Tuscaloosa: University of Alabama Press, 1984.

Doyno, Victor A. *Writing "Huck Finn": Mark Twain's Creative Process*. Philadelphia: University of Pennsylvania Press, 1992.

Emerson, Everett. *Mark Twain: A Literary Life*. Philadelphia: University of Pennsylvania Press, 1999.

Fishkin, Shelley Fisher, ed. *A Historical Guide to Mark Twain*, New York: Oxford University Press, 2002.

———. *Lighting Out for the Territory: Reflections of Mark Twain and American Culture*. New York: Oxford University Press, 1998.

———. *Was Huck Black? Mark Twain and African American Voices*. New York: Oxford University Press, 1993.

Fulton, Joe B. *Mark Twain in the Margins: The Quarry Farm Marginalia and A Connecticut Yankee in King Arthur's Court*, Tuscaloosa: University of Alabama Press, 2000.

Gillman, Susan, and Forrest G. Robinson. *Mark Twain's "Pudd'nhead Wilson": Race, Conflict, and Culture*. Durham, N.C.: Duke University Press, 1990.

Graff, Gerald and James Phelan, eds. *Adventures of Huckleberry Finn: A Case Study in Critical Controversy*. New York: Bedford/St. Martin's, 1995.

Harris, Susan K. *The Courtship of Olivia Langdon and Mark Twain*. Cambridge: Cambridge University Press, 1996.

Howells, William Dean. *My Mark Twain: Reminiscences and Criticisms*. New York: Harper & Brothers, 1910.

Hutchinson, Stuart, ed. *Mark Twain: Critical Assessments*. 4 vols. Robertsbridge, East Sussex, U.K.: Helm Information Ltd., 1993.

Inge, M. Thomas, ed. *Huck Finn Among the Critics: A Centennial Selection*. Frederick, Md.: University Publications of America, 1985.

Jerome, Robert D., and Herbert A. Wisbey Jr., eds. *Mark Twain in Elmira*. Elmira, N.Y.: Mark Twain Society, Inc., 1977.

Kahn, Sholom J. *Mark Twain's Mysterious Stranger: A Study of the Manuscript Texts*. Columbia: University of Missouri Press, 1978.

Kaplan, Fred. *The Singular Mark Twain*. New York: Doubleday, 2003.

Kaplan, Justin. *Mr. Clemens and Mark Twain: A Biography*. 1966. Reprint, New York: Touchstone, 1991.

Knoper, Randall. *Acting Naturally: Mark Twain in the Culture of Performance*. Berkeley and Los Angeles: University of California Press, 1995.

Langdon, Jervis. *Samuel Langhorne Clemens: Some Reminiscences and Some Excerpts from Letters and unpublished Manuscripts*. Elmira, N.Y.: Privately printed, 1935.

Lawton, Mary. *A Lifetime with Mark Twain: The Memories of Katy Leary, for Thirty Years His Faithful and Devoted Servant*. New York: Harcourt, Brace & Co., 1925.

Leonard, James S., ed. *Making Mark Twain Work in the Classroom*. Durham, N.C.: Duke University Press, 1999.

——— et al., eds. *Satire or Evasion? Black Perspectives on Huckleberry Finn*, Durham, N.C.: Duke University Press, 1992.

Leonard, James S., Thomas A. Tenney, and Thadious M. Davis. *Satire or Evasion? Black Perspectives on "Huckleberry Finn."* Durham, N.C.: Duke University Press, 1991.

Lorch, Fred W. *The Trouble Begins at Eight. Mark Twain's Lecture Tours.* Ames: Iowa State University Press, 1968.

Meltzer, Milton. *Mark Twain Himself: A Pictorial Biography,* St. Louis: University of Missouri Press, 2002.

Mensh, Elaine, and Harry Mensh. *Black, White, and Huckleberry Finn: Re-Imagining the American Dream.* Tuscaloosa: University of Alabama Press, 2000.

Paine, Albert Bigelow. *Mark Twain: A Biography: The Personal and Literary Life of Samuel Langhorne Clemens.* 4 vols. New York: Harper & Brothers, 1912.

Richardson, Robert. "Annette," in *Willow and Wattle.* 1893. Available online: http://www.twainquotes.com/headstone.html. Accessed 27 April 2004.

Robinson, Forrest, ed. *The Cambridge Companion to Mark Twain.* Cambridge: Cambridge University Press, 1995.

Sattelmeyer, Robert, and J. Donald Crowley. *One Hundred Years of "Huckleberry Finn": The Boy, His Book and American Culture.* Columbia: University of Missouri Press, 1985.

Scharnhorst, Gary, ed. *Critical Essays on "The Adventures of Tom Sawyer."* New York: G.K. Hall, 1993.

Skandera-Trombley, Laura E. *Mark Twain in the Company of Women,* Philadelphia: University of Pennsylvania Press, 1997.

Skandera-Trombley, Laura E., and Michael J. Kiskis, eds., *Constructing Mark Twain: New Directions in Scholarship,* St. Louis: University of Missouri Press, 2002.

Simpson, Claude M., ed. *Twentieth Century Interpretations of Adventures of Huckleberry Finn: A Collection of Critical Essays.* Englewood Cliffs, N.J.: Prentice-Hall, 1968.

Sloane, David E. E., ed. *Mark Twain's Humor: Critical Essays.* New York: Garland, 1993.

Smith, Henry Nash, ed. *Mark Twain: A Collection of Critical Essays.* Englewood Cliffs, N.J.: Prentice-Hall, 1963.

Sundquist, Eric J., ed. *Mark Twain: A Collection of Critical Essays.* Englewood Cliffs, N.J.: Prentice-Hall, 1994.

Ward, Geoffrey C., Dayton Duncan, and Ken Burns, *Mark Twain: An Illustrated Biography,* New York: Knopf, 2001.

REFERENCE WORKS

Camfield, Gregg. *The Oxford Reader's Companion to Mark Twain,* New York: Oxford University Press, 2002.

Gribben, Alan. *Mark Twain's Library: A Reconstruction*. 2 vols. Boston: G.K. Hall & Co., 1980.

Johnson, Merle. *Mark Twain: A Bibliography*. New York: Harper & Brothers, 1935.

LeMaster, J.R. and James D. Wilson. *The Mark Twain Encyclopedia*. New York: Garland, 1993.

Rasmussen, R. Kent. *Mark Twain A–Z: The Essential Reference to His Life and Writings*. New York: Oxford University Press, 1996.

DVDS AND VIDEOS

A&E Biography. *Biography: Mark Twain*, A & E Entertainment, (VHS), 1999.

Burns, Ken, dir. *Ken Burns's Mark Twain*, PBS Home Video, (DVD or VHS), 2002.

Holbrook, Hal, perf. *Mark Twain Tonight!*, Kultur Video, (VHS), 1999.

ELECTRONIC AND INTERNET SOURCES

University of California at Berkeley. *The Mark Twain Papers & Project*. Online archive of correspondence and other materials. http://bancroft.berkeley.edu/MTP/

Burns, Ken et al. and PBS. *Mark Twain: Known by Everyone—Liked by All*. Web site linked to the Ken Burns documentary, *Mark Twain*. http://www.pbs.org/marktwain/index.html

INDEX

Abolition, 26
Adventures of Huckleberry Finn, 3, 16, 17, 24, 50, 63, 69, 70–74, 80, 84, 91
The Adventures of Tom Sawyer, 16, 17, 18, 36, 63, 66, 68–70
African Americans, 2, 3, 9, 11, 50, 72–73, 80
Amant, Joseph P., 21, 22
Amazon River, 29–31, 51
American literature, 68, 69, 79, 80, 103
American Publishing Company, 59, 65, 69
Ancestry, 5–6
Angelfish, 98–99
Angel's Camp, California, 43–44
Antenne Collection, Mark Twain Archive, Elmira, 80
Aquarium Club, 99
The Atlantic Monthly, 78
Aunt Polly (character), 69
Australia, 48

Bates, Edward, 39
Beecher, Henry Ward, 51
Beecher, Thomas K., 62
Beecher, Thomas Ward, 65
Bermuda, 99, 101
Billiards, 68
Bixby, Horace, 31–33
Blankenship, Tom, 17, 69, 72
Bliss, Elisha, 61, 77
Boston Carpet-Bag, 23
Boston Lyceum Bureau, 48
Bowen, Will, 17, 69
Briggs, John, 17
Brooklyn, New York, 51
Brown, William, 33–34
Buffalo Express, 57–61
Buffalo, New York, 49, 57–61, 64

Calaveras County, California, 43–44
California, 43–51
Canada, 48
Carleton, George W., 44, 45–46

Carson City, Nevada, 40–41, 47, 51
Cats, 76
Champ, Neal, 17
Charles L. Webster and Company, 64, 89, 91
Choice Humorous Works, 68
Christian Science, 96
Civil War, 37, 48, 88, 91
Clapp, Henry, 44
Clemens, Benjamin (brother), 8, 13, 15
Clemens, Clara Langdon (daughter), 66, 74, 79–80, 95, 98, 99
Clemens, Flavius, 5
Clemens, Gregory, 5
Clemens, Henry (brother), 12, 17, 22–23, 33–36, 65, 69
Clemens, James (cousin), 16
Clemens, Jane Lampton (mother), 6–7, 9, 11, 13, 16, 21, 25, 57, 60, 69
Clemens, Jane (Jean) Lampton (daughter), 74, 95, 99–101
Clemens, Jane Montgomery (maternal grandmother), 6
Clemens, John Marshall (father), birth and childhood, 5–6; character, 8; death, 19, 90
Clemens, Langdon (son), 60, 65
Clemens, Margaret (sister), 12, 65
Clemens, (Mollie) Eleanor Stotts (sister-in-law), 29
Clemens, Olivia (Livy) Louise Langdon (wife), 53–55, 57–85, 91; death, 94–95
Clemens, Olivia Susan (Susy) (daughter), 65, 74; death, 92–94
Clemens, Orion (brother), 7, 12, 22–25, 39, 57, 60, 94
Clemens, Pamela. *See* Moffett, Pamela Clemens
Clemens, Pope X, 5
Clemens, Pope XI, 5
Clemens, Samuel (paternal grandfather), 5
Clemens, Samuel Langhorne, 1, ancestry, 5–6; birth, 8–9; family and friendships, 74–79; pseudonym, 41–43; school days, 14–19; steamboat pilot days, 31–37
Cleveland, Ohio, 48
Colonel Crossman (steamboat), 31
A Connecticut Yankee in King Arthur's Court, 36, 64, 68
Coon, Ben, 44
Cooper Union, 47–48
Cord, Mary Ann, 79–80
Crane, Susan Langdon (sister-in-law), 54, 59, 62–63, 65, 74
Crane, Theodore (brother-in-law), 54

Date, 1601, 68
David Copperfield (Dickens), 54
Dawson's Landing (fictional town), 89
Dickens, Charles, 50, 53
Doubling, 3, 43, 89
Douglass, Frederick, 55

Eddy, Mary Baker, 96
"Ellerslie" (Quarry Farm playhouse), 63
Elmira, New York, 53, 54, 57, 64, 65, 71, 81, 94, 101
Emerson, Ralph Waldo, 24, 94
England, 6, 93
Esmeralda, Nevada, 40–41

Exploration of the Valley of the Amazon (U.S. Navy), 29
Europe, 48

Fairbanks, Mary Mason, 52–53, 57, 60, 77
Florence, Italy, 95
Florida, Missouri, 8
Franklin, Benjamin, 27, 29, 47, 90
Fredonia, New York, 60, 74
Fuller, Frank, 47

Gabrilowitsch, Ossip (son-in-law), 100, 102
The Gilded Age, 7, 57, 65, 68, 70
Glassock Island, 17, 24
Gleason, Dr. Rachel Brooks, 60
Gleason, Dr. Silas O., 60
Goggin, Pamela (paternal grandmother), 5
Goodman, Joe, 41, 43, 55
Grant, Ulysses S., 77, 91
Gribben, Alan, 94
Griffin, George, 79, 80–81

Halley's Comet, 9, 102
Hannibal, Missouri, 12–14, 23, 26, 63, 69, 94
Hannibal Daily Journal, 24
Hannibal Gazette, 21
Hannibal *Journal*, 22
Hannibal Tri-Weekly Messenger, 24
Harper, Joe (character), 69
Harte, Bret, 46, 78
Hartford, Connecticut, 49, 58, 64–68, 69
Hartford Courant, 64
The Hartford House, 65–68, 90
Hawaii, 43, 46, 52
Hawkins, Laura, 18–19, 69
Hemingway, Ernest, 72, 103
Holiday's Hill, Hannibal, 13
Holmes, Oliver Wendell, 24
Holy Land, 51
Horr, Miss (teacher), 14–15
Howells, William Dean, 63, 78–79, 100, 102
Huckleberry, 70–71

India, 48
Injun Joe (character), 70
Innocents Abroad, 43, 51–53, 58, 61, 78

Jackson's Island, 71
Jamestown, New York, 49
Jennie (slave), 9, 10, 13, 15
Jim (character), 71, 80–81
Joan of Arc, 22, 30
Jude the Obscure (Hardy), 101
"The Jumping Frog Story," 43
The Jungle Book (Kipling), 83
Just So Stories (Kipling), 83, 84

Kaplan, Justin, 43
Kentucky, 2, 6
Keokuk, Iowa, 29–30, 47
Keokuk Post, 30
Kim (Kipling), 84
Kipling, Rudyard, 81–84, 98

Lampton, Jane. *See* Clemens, Jane Lampton
Langdon, Charles Jervis (Charley), 52, 59, 81
Langdon, Jervis (father-in-law), 53, 58, 62
Langdon, Olivia Lewis (mother-in-law), 53, 65
Langdon, Olivia Louise. *See* Clemens, Olivia Louise Langdon

Lawton, Mary, 79
Leary, Katy, 79–80, 93, 95, 99
Leary, Mary, 79
Lecture tours, 46–51
Lewis, John T., 81, 94
Life on the Mississippi, 36, 39, 64, 68, 73, 81
A Lifetime with Mark Twain, (Leary), 79
Lincoln, Abraham, 37, 39, 79
London, England, 48, 97, 98
Louisville, Kentucky, 30
Lover's Leap, Hannibal, 13
Lowell, Robert, 24
Lyon, Isabel, 100

Maguire's Opera House, 46
Mark Twain Company, 42
Mark Twain in the Company of Women (Skandera-Trombley), 75–76
Mark Twain Papers Project, 73
Mark Twain's (Burlesque) Autobiography, 68
Mary (slave), 11
McCormick, Wales, 21
McDowell, Dr., 18
McHenry, Jerry, 26
McMurry, Pet, 21
McReynolds, John, 26
Mediterranean Sea, 51, 52
Memphis, Tennessee, 34
Middle Ages, 5
Miller, Joaquin, 46
Missouri, 47, 70
Missouri *Courier*, 21
Mississippi River, 2, 12, 17, 31–37, 60, 88
Moffett, Annie (niece), 57
Moffett, Pamela Clemens (sister), 7, 13, 25, 57, 60
Moffett, William Anderson, 25
Morgan, Hank (character), 36
Muscatine, Iowa, 28
Muscatine *Journal*, 27
My Mark Twain (Howells), 79

Native Americans, 2, 6
Nevada, 39–43
New Jersey, 5
New Orleans, Louisiana, 30, 37
New Orleans *Picayune*, 42
New York, New York, 25–27, 47–48, 97, 102
New Zealand, 48
Nook Farm, 65
North America, 48, 70
North American Review, 45
Number One: Mark Twain's Sketches, 68
Nye, Emma, 60

Octagonal study, Quarry Farm, 62–63, 74, 80
Othello (Shakespeare), 28
Oxford University, 2, 98

Paige Compositor typesetter, 28, 89, 92
Paine, Albert Bigelow, 68, 100, 101
Papa: An Intimate Portrait (Susy Clemens), 76–77
Paul Jones (steamboat), 30
Pennsylvania (steamboat), 33
Petersburg (fictional town), 69–70, 71
Peyton, Dr., 35
Philadelphia American Courier, 23
Philadelphia Inquirer, 27
Philadelphia, Penn., 27–28, 90

Plain Tales from the Hills (Kipling), 83
Politics, 96–97
Pony Express, 40
Potter, Edward Tuckerman, 65
The Prince and the Pauper, 64, 68, 89
Pudd'nhead Wilson, 43, 81, 88–90
Punch, Brothers, Punch!, 68

Quaker City (steamboat), 51–53, 57, 77, 98
Quarleses's Farm, 8, 10–11, 13, 15, 22, 64, 95
Quarles, John A., 8, 10–11
Quarles, Patsey Ann Lampton (aunt), 8
Quarry Farm, Elmira, 59, 61–64, 73, 74, 80, 94

Race, 3, 71, 80, 104
Redding, Connecticut, 99–103
Redpath, James, 48, 49
Religion, 96–97
Rockwell, Norman, 69
Roughing It, 40, 44, 46, 60, 61, 63, 65, 68

Sacramento Union, 46
St. Joseph, Missouri, 40
St. Louis, Missouri, 21, 25, 37, 49
St. Louis Evening News, 25, 29
St. Louis Republican, 29
Sandwich Islands. *See* Hawaii
San Francisco, California, 43–46, 50, 51, 55
San Francisco Alta California, 46, 51, 71
San Francisco Call, 43, 46
San Francisco Dramatic Chronicle, 46
San Francisco Trade Union, 46
The Saturday Post, 30
Sawyer, Sid (character), 35, 69
Screamers, 68
Self-pasting scrapbook, 90–91
Sellers, Isaiah, 42
Sketches New and Old, 68
Slavery, 16, 80, 88
Slaves, 9, 10, 80
Smiley, Jim (character), 44
Snodgrass, Thomas Jefferson, 30
"Sociable Jimmy," 72–73
South Africa, 48
Stage technique, 48–49
Steamboats, 31–37
The Stolen White Elephant, 68
Stoddard, Charles Warren, 46
Stormfield, 99–103
Stowe, Harriet Beecher, 65
Suetonius, 5
Syracuse, New York, 26

Taft, William, President, 102
"Tar Baby" (Uncle Remus), 50
Taylor, Annie, 29
"The Tennessee Land," 7, 24
Thatcher, Becky (character), 18, 69, 73, 82
Tolstoy, Leo, 91
Tom Sawyer (character), 82
Tom Sawyer, Detective, 69
Tom Sawyer Abroad, 69
A Tramp Abroad, 64, 68
"The Trouble Begins at Eight," 47
The Trouble Begins at Eight (Lorch), 50
"A True Story," 80
A True Story and the Recent Carnival of Crime, 68
Tuolumne County, California, 43–44

Twain, Mark (pseudonym), 1, 3, 33, 41–43
Twichell, Joseph, 57, 77–78, 102

Uncle Dan'l, 9
Uncle Remus tales, 50
Underground Railroad, 55
United States, 48

Virginia, 5, 9
Virginia City Territorial Enterprise, 41
Voice, 2, 3

Ward, Artemus, 44
Warner, C. D. (Charles Dudley), 57, 65, 68, 84
Was Huck Black? (Fishkin), 72
Washington, D.C., 28, 48, 97
Water Cure, Elmira, 60
Webb, Charles Henry, 45, 46
Webster, Dan'l (character), 44
West Point Military Academy, 50
What Is Man?, 79
White suits, 97
Whitman, Walt, 91, 103
Williams, True, 69
Wolf, Jim, 23
Women and women's rights, 2, 74–76
Woodlawn Cemetery, 65, 103
World's Fair, 26, 90

Yale University, 3